信山社双書
実際編

WTO紛争処理の一断面

――協定解釈と「辞書」の利用――

袁　田

信　山　社

はしがき

2008年中国の自動車部品の輸入に関連する措置事件は，中国が世界貿易機関に加入した後の最初の敗訴として，大きな波紋を巻き起こしました．多くの中国の研究者が論文を書き，中国の措置やパネル，上級委員会の判断について検討しました．私は，中国研究者が書いた論文とパネルや上級委員会の報告書から，条約の用語を解釈する方法に相違があることに気づきました．

例としては，中国の措置が，「GATT協定」第2条の関税措置であるか，あるいは，「GATT協定」第3条の内国税措置であるのかを判断する際，中国の研究者のほとんどは，関税や内国税の特徴を議論し，中国の措置の性質を判断しました．ところが，パネルは，中国の研究者とは全く違う方法で，解釈の道を探っていました．パネルは，まず辞書を調べ，字義を確認した後，「GATT協定」の文脈を読み解き，関税と内国税とを定義しました．その後で，「GATT協定」第2条と第3条を読み，その目的を確認し，最後に，中国の措置が「GATT協定」第3条によるものであることを認定したのです．

パネルはなぜこのような方法で，「GATT協定」を解釈したのでしょうか．資料を通してわかったのは，パネルや上級委員会が，長期間の実践を通して，条約についての独特の解釈体系を持ち合わせているということでした．GATT／WTOの発展とともに，紆余曲折を経て，この解釈の体系が築き上げられてきました．

私は最初，この独特の解釈体系全体について検討するつもりでした．条約解釈は少なからぬ事件において様々な紛争を解決するための基礎となっており，紛争を解決していく上で，きわめて重要なものであると言えるからです．しかし，研究を進めるうちに，しだいにこのテーマの大きさを認識しました．結局，私は，この解釈体系の第一歩となる辞書の利用についての分析を行うことにしました．この本は，その最初の研究成果をまとめたものです．

さて，本書の出版にあたって，私はまず指導教官たる石黒一憲先生に，深く感謝申し上げます．先生を中心とした自由闊達な思考ができる環境，謹厳実直な学術研究の雰囲気，そして先生の熱心な指導がなければ，本書の出版はとても考えることができませんでした．また，お世話になった諸先生方，友人，家族にもお礼を申し上げます．皆様のお陰で，わたしの研究生活は，楽しく幸せなものになりました．

最後に，本書が少しでも皆様のお役に立つことができれば，幸いです．

2012 年 8 月

袁　田

目　次

WTO紛争処理の一断面

―協定解釈と「辞書」の利用―

はじめに

2010年7月，台湾国立大学法学院教授Chang-Fa Loは，オックスフォード大学出版局の国際紛争処理誌（Journal of International Dispute Settlement）で“Good Faith Use of Dictionary in the Search of Ordinary Meaning under the WTO Dispute Settlement Understanding”という論文を発表した．Lo教授はこの論文を通して，世界貿易機関（以下，WTOと呼ぶ．）の紛争処理手続きにおける辞書の利用について自己の見解を提示した[(1)]．そして，今年の1月，Lo教授のこの論文に対して，Isabelle Van Damme博士が同じ雑誌で“On‘Good Faith Use of Dictionary in the Search of Ordinary Meaning under the WTO Dispute Settlement Understanding’— A Reply to Professor Chang-Fa Lo”という論文を発表して，異なる意見を主張した[(2)]．Lo教授は，2011年の7月，再度“A Clearer Rule for Dictionary Use Will Not Affect Holistic Approach and Flexibility of Treaty Interpretation — A Rejoinder to Dr Isabelle Van Damme”という論文によって，Van Damme博士の論文に答えた[(3)]．彼らが辞書で用語の意味を調べるという一見非常に簡単なことに重大な関心を寄せている原因は，何であろうか．

---

(1) Chang-Fa Lo, Good Faith Use of Dictionary in the Search of Ordinary Meaning under the WTO Dispute Settlement Understanding , Journal of International Dispute Settlement, Vol. 1, No. 2 (2010), at 431-445.

(2) Isabelle Van Damme, Journal of International Dispute Settlement, Vol. 2, No. 1 (2011), at 231-239.

(3) Chang-Fa Lo, J. Int. Disp. Settlement (2011), first published online July 23, 2011 doi:10.1093/jnlids/idr013.

2011年2月までに422件のWTOの紛争事件で採択された160件のパネルの報告書のうち，141件が辞書を利用した[4]．91件の上級委員会の報告書の中にも，辞書を利用したものが60件あった．最初の100件の紛争事件（WT/DS1/R - WT/DS100/R）の中で，辞書が利用されなかったのは12件であったが，その後の300件（WT/DS101/R - WT/DS400/R）の中で，辞書が利用されなかった紛争事件はわずか4件であった[5]．また，最初は1件のパネルの報告書の中で辞書での意味が利用される用語は1つか2つしかなかったが，最近のものでは数十箇所に至った（資料3を参照）．紛争事件について議論するとき，紛争当事国であれ，第三国であれ，パネルであれ，上級委員会であれ，皆が皆辞書の意味を根拠として自己の意見を主張するようになった．

辞書は，WTOの「紛争処理に関する規則及び手続に関する了解」（Understanding on Rules and Procedures Governing the Settlement of Disputes，以下DSUという）の付録に列記された締約国の権利と義務を規律する協定ではなく，また紛争処理手続きにおいてパネルや上級委員会が利用できる法源でもない．それにもかかわら

---

(4) パネルの報告書の中で，辞書が利用されなかったのは，WT/DS2/R；WT/DS4/R；WT/DS22/R；WT/DS24/R；WT/DS26/R；WT/DS31/R；WT/DS58/R；WT/DS60/R；WT/DS62/R；WT/DS67/R；WT/DS68/R；WT/DS87/R；WT/DS110/R；WT/DS212/R；WT/DS323/R；WT/DS331/R；WT/DS344/R；WT/DS383/R；WT/DS402/Rである．

WTO紛争事件の履行確認関連のパネル報告書と上級委員会報告書については，本稿では扱っていないが，今後の検討の対象としたい．

(5) 総件数については経済産業省通商政策局編の「紛争案件一覧」参照．『2011年版不公正貿易報告書』http://www.meti.go.jp/committee/summary/0004532/2011_houkoku01.html

以下，本論文では，WTO公式ホームページからダウンロードした報告書によって統計を行う．

http://docsonline.wto.org/gen_home.asp?language=1&_=1

ず，なぜWTOの紛争処理手続きにおいてこれほど頻繁に利用されるのか[6]．また辞書が頻繁に利用されることは紛争処理手続きにどんな影響を与えるのか．本書はこれらの問題を検討する．

本書の構成は以下の通りである．まず第Ⅰ章においては，WTO紛争処理手続きの背景を分析した上で，辞書が利用される根拠を探求する．第Ⅱ章においては，実例を通してWTO紛争処理手続きにおける辞書の利用の実態を提示しながら，「辞書の利用」が論争の焦点になる原因を探求する．第Ⅲ章では，辞書と関わるいくつかの問題点を分析する．第Ⅳ章で，上級委員会が紛争事件報告書を通じて示した辞書の利用についての意見と，Lo教授が論文の中で示した8つのルールを分析する．そして，最後に，以上の結論を示すこととする．なお巻末には，2010年までのWTOの各紛争事件のパネル報告書と上級委員会報告書において利用された辞書のリスト（資料1および2）と，辞書が利用された用語のリスト（資料3および4）を，本書の参考資料として掲記した．

(6) Lo, supra note 1, at 431.

第Ⅰ章　紛争処理手続きにおいて辞書が利用される背景と原因

パネルの報告書における辞書の利用の歴史をさかのぼると，意外な事実に気づく．もとより漏れはありうるが，筆者が調べた限りでは，GATT 時代に紛争解決手続で辞書が利用された事例は，意外なまでに少ないのである[(1)]．むしろ，辞書の利用は，WTO 設立後，とくに 1999 年以降（本書 17 頁で後述する）において急速に顕在化した現象と，言ってよいであろう．それゆえ，まず背景として，GATT から WTO への紛争処理手続きの発展を見る．

---

(1)　WTO のホームページで公開された 127 件の GATT パネル報告書 (GATT Panel Report) の中で，「辞書」（dictionary）をキーワードとして検索した結果，「辞書」（dictionary）を利用したのは，以下の 6 件である（アクセス：2012 年 1 月 15 日）．

GATT Panel Report, EEC Restrictions on Imports of Apples from Chile, L/5047, BISD 27S/98, 10 November 1980, at 10, para.3.24; GATT Panel Report, Anti-Dumping Duties on Imports of Polyacetal Resins from the United States, ADP/92, 2 April 1993, at 36, note 34; GATT Panel Report, United States - Measures Affecting Imports of Softwood Lumber from Canada, SCM/162, 27 October 1993, at 26, note 30; GATT Panel Report, United States - Imposition of Anti-dumping Duties on Imports of Fresh and Chilled Atlantic Salmon From Norway, ADP/87, 27 April 1994, at 23, note 56 & at 24, para.87; GATT Panel Report, United States - Imposition of Countervailing Duties on Imports of Fresh and Chilled Atlantic Salmon From Norway, SCM/153, 28 April 1994, at 20, note 53 & at 21, para.62；GATT Panel Report, United States - Imposition of Countervailing Duties on Certain Hot-Rolled Lead and Bismuth Carbon-Steel Products Originating in France, Germany and the United Kingdom, SCM/185, 15 November 1994, at 20ff, para.60, para.66 & at 168, note 173.

1　背景：紛争処理手続き（GATT から WTO へ）

WTO は，国際貿易に関するルールを取り扱う唯一の国際機関であり(2)，また経済面における最も重要な国際機関でもある．2011 年 5 月 13 日に日本が発表した 2011 年版の不公正貿易報告書によれば，2011 年 3 月時点での WTO の加盟国は 153 カ国である(3)．そして，30 カ国が WTO に加盟申請中である(4)．WTO は，最も重要な貿易面での国際機構として，その影響力を更に拡大しつつある．

ところが，WTO の前身である GATT（関税と貿易に関する一般協定．以下 GATT と呼ぶ）は国際組織ではなく，関税の引き下げや貿易障壁の削減を目的とした暫定協定にすぎなかった．第二次世界大戦後，大戦に勝利した連合国は，戦前の閉鎖的な経済（保護主義）が世界の経済活動を縮小させ，国際的な対立を激化させたことで戦争を引き起こしたとの反省から，国際協力と自由貿易をめざす新体制を作ることになった(5)．しかし，既に第二次大戦末期に開催

---

(2)　WTO 公式ホームページには，“The World Trade Organization (WTO) is the only global international organization dealing with the rules of trade between nations.” とある．
http://www.wto.org/english/thewto_e/whatis_e/whatis_e.htm

(3)　前掲「はじめに」注(5)『2011 年版不公正貿易報告書』779 頁．http://www.meti.go.jp/policy/trade_policy/wto_compliance_report/index.html WTO のホームページに今現在載っている加盟国数は『2011 年版不公正貿易報告書』に記載された数と同じであるが，前者の日付は 2008 年 7 月 23 日である．http://www.wto.org/english/thewto_e/whatis_e/tif_e/org6_e.htm アクセス：2011 年 11 月 6 日．

(4)　前掲「はじめに」注(5)『2011 年版不公正貿易報告書』781 頁．

(5)　対外経済政策総合サイト (http://www.meti.go.jp/policy/trade_policy/wto/negotiation/doha/wto-index.html)，及び，John H. Jackson,The Jurisprudence of GATT & the WTO, Cambridge University Press (2007), at 21.

されたブレトン・ウッズ会議において国際通貨基金（International Monetary Fund: IMF）及び世界銀行（国際復興開発銀行［International Bank of Reconstruction and Development］）を設置することが合意されていたものの，貿易面における国際機関の設置はスムーズにいかなかった．戦後米国の主導で国連の下に国際貿易機関（International Trade Organization: ITO）を設置する試みがなされ，国際貿易機関憲章が起草されて多くの国の署名を得たが，米国議会の批准拒否にあって結局発効しなかった．

GATTはこの空白を埋めるために1947年に締結されたが，その本来の性格は暫定協定であり，国際貿易機関憲章が発効した暁にはこれに吸収されるべきものとされていた．しかし，国際貿易機関憲章は結局発効せず，GATTは1995年1月1日にWTO憲章（世界貿易機関憲章）が発効するまで国際貿易の実質的な「憲法」として機能したのであった(6)．

暫定協定として締結されたGATT協定は，22条と23条で，貿易紛争の処理について簡単に定めている．つまり，どういう状況下で協議の申立てを行うことができるかを規定している．具体的な紛争処理手続きについての規定はなかったが，GATTでは長年の実践を通して一連の紛争処理手続きが定着することになった(7)．以上の実践から生じた紛争処理手続きについての慣行は，東京ラウンドで「通報，協議，紛争処理及び監視に関する了解事項」として成文化され，この了解事項は1979年11月の締約国団会議において「決定」として採択された(8)．1986年よりウルグアイ・ラウンド（1986

(6) 松下満雄＝清水章雄＝中川淳司『ガット・WTO法』（有斐閣，2000）1頁（松下）．

(7) David Palmeter and Petros C.Mavroidis, Dispute Settlement in the World Trade Organization 2nd.ed.Cambridge University Press (2004), at 8. 清水章雄「ガットの紛争処理手続き」商学討究（小樽商科大学）34巻2号108-113頁をも参照．

(8) 清水・前掲注(7) 106頁．

年-1994年）が行われ，1995年1月1日WTOが発足した．それとともに，紛争処理手続きも大きく一歩前進し，独特で，大きな成果だが，しかし議論の多い（unique, a great achievement, controversial...）システム(9)が現れた．

従来のGATT時代の紛争処理手続きと比べて，主要な特徴としては，以下の3つがあげられる．第一に，GATT時代にはダンピング防止協定，補助金協定，関税評価協定，スタンダード協定及び政府調達協定等に分散していた紛争処理に関する規定が，WTO協定の附属書2に該当するDSUに統一された．第二に，締約国団のコンセンサスによるというGATT時代のパネル報告の採択方式を改めて，パネル報告及び上級委員会報告の採択は紛争処理機関における「逆コンセンサス方式」によって行うこととした．このような変化によって，GATT時代のように敗訴加盟国が自己に不利な報告の採択をブロックすることはできなくなり，パネル報告及び上級委員会報告は全員一致の反対がない限り採択されるようになった．第三に，WTO紛争処理手続きでは二審制が導入された．第一審に相当するのがパネルであるが，第二審に相当するのが上級委員会である．出されたパネルの報告書に不服な当事国は上級委員会に上訴できる(10)．このような変化は紛争処理の効率を向上させ，紛争当事国がWTOの紛争処理手続きを利用するインセンティブを高めることとなった．2011年2月までにWTOの紛争処理手続きを利用した紛争事件は422件であり，また，2010年に協議要請を提起した案件は17件であった(11)．王冠上の宝石（jewel in its crown）と称賛されたWTO紛争処理手続きは，重要な役割を果たし続けてい

(9) John H. Jackson, Sovereignty, the WTO, and Changing Fundamentals of International Law, Cambridge University Press (2006), at 135.

(10) 松下＝清水＝中川・前掲注(6)3頁（松下）．

(11) 前掲「はじめに」注(5)『2011年版不公正貿易報告書』450頁の図表16-3.

る[12].

2　辞書の利用の根拠 ―「通常の意味」を確定する重要な方法

(1)「解釈に関する国際法上の慣習的規則」―ウィーン条約法条約31条と32条[13]

WTOの紛争事件は，主にある国の政策や規定がWTOの協定に違反するかどうかをめぐって展開されたものである．それを議論する前提として，まず関係する協定の条項の意味を解釈しなければならない．GATT時代において，関税及び貿易に関する一般協定，ダンピング防止協定（関税及び貿易に関する一般協定第6条の実施に関する協定）や補助金協定（関税及び貿易に関する一般協定第6条，第16条，第23条の解釈及び適用に関する協定）等には，条約の解釈についての規則はなかった．パネルの委員には外交官出身の人が多いため[14]，条約を解釈する際に，条約を起草するときの準備作業（travaux preparatoires）を勘案することが多かった．WTOが発足した後，DSU3条2項で「加盟国は，同制度が対象協定に基づく加盟国の権利及び義務を維持し並びに解釈に関する国際法上の慣習的規則に従って対象協定の現行の規定の解釈を明らかにすることに資するものであることを認識する.」[15]と定められ，この条項がパネ

---

(12) Jackson, supra note 15, at 135.

(13) ウィーン条約法条約の日本語訳は奥脇直也編『国際条約集』（有斐閣，2009）119-128頁を参照した．

(14)「小委員会の委員は公務員であることが望ましいとされているが，例外的に非公務員が委員となったこともある．通常はGATTの常駐代表又は締約国の中央官庁の公務員の中から選ばれ，実際には北欧諸国及びスイスの出身であることが多い」清水・前掲注(7) 121頁注(63).

(15) DSUの日本語訳は小寺彰＝中川淳司編『基本経済条約集』（有斐閣，2009）118-131頁を参照した．

ルの条約解釈の基準になったのである．しかし，「解釈に関する国際法上の慣習的規則」というのは，一体どういう意味であるか，明確には定められていない．

ウィーン条約法条約は，国際連合国際法委員会（ILC）が，慣習法であった条約法を条約の形に法典化したものである．1969年5月にウィーンで採択されたが，条約の84条において「この条約は，35番目の批准書又は加入書が寄託された日の後30日目の日に効力を生ずる．」と定められており，1980年1月に発効した．現在126カ国が署名しており，111カ国が条約の当事国である(16)．153ヵ国のWTOの加盟国の中には，ウィーン条約法条約の当事国ではない，つまり，ウィーン条約法条約に拘束されていない国がいまだにたくさんあるが，ウィーン条約法条約の中の条約解釈についての原則は，諸国に認められ，紛争処理の中で広範に利用された．GATT時代の紛争事件の報告書ではウィーン条約法条約には言及されていなかったが(17)，WTOが発足した後の第1番目の報告書，つまり米国

⑯　国連のデータより．アクセス：2011年8月24日．http://treaties.un.org/pages/ViewDetailsIII.aspx?&src=UNTSONLINE&mtdsg_no=XXIII~1&chapter=23&Temp=mtdsg3&lang=en

⑰　「米国のカナダ産軟材の輸入に影響を与える措置事件のパネル報告では，ウィーン条約法条約31条1項と同一の表現を条約解釈に関する国際法の慣習的原則としているが，同条約それ自体には言及していない．」とするのは，清水章雄「WTO紛争解決における解釈手法の展開と問題点」日本国際経済法学会年報第19号（法律文化社，2010年）23頁注⑽．なお，この点につき一次資料を念のため示しておく．そこには，“The Panel thus proceeded to consider the meaning of the term "sufficient evidence" in Article 2:1 guided by the customary principles of international law on treaty interpretation, according to which treaty terms were to be given their ordinary meaning in their context and in the light of the treaty's object and purpose.” とある．(GATT Panel Report, United States-Measures Affecting Imports of Softwood Lumber from Canada, SCM/162, adopted 27 October 1993, BISD 40S/358, at 95, para. 330.)．

ーガソリン基準事件の報告書の中で，パネルはGATT第3条を解釈するためにウィーン条約法条約の31条を利用した[18]．上級委員会は，その問題について「31条【解釈に関する一般的な規則】は，『条約は，文脈により且つその趣旨及び目的に照らして与えられる用語の通常の意味に従い誠実に解釈するものとする.』とした．この主旨は，本件のすべての当事国及び第三国に採用され，この『解釈に関する一般的な規則』は伝統的な解釈方法，かつ国際慣習法として見なされたのである．従って，その規則はDSU 3条2項の『解釈に関する国際法上の慣習的規則』の一部分と見なすべきであり，世界貿易機関設立マラケシュ協定及び附属書としての一連の適用協定の解釈のために遵守される」[19]と，確認したのである．

日本の酒税事件でも，パネルは「解釈の補足的な手段の役割に関するウィーン条約法条約32条も，31条と同じく，DSU 3条2項の『解釈に関する国際法上の慣習的規則』である.」と述べ[20]，上級委員会もこれに賛意を表したのである[21]．

その後，パネルや上級委員会は，報告書で条約を解釈するにあたってウィーン条約法条約の31条，32条を，繰り返し強調してきた．かくて，ウィーン条約法条約の31条，32条はすでに「WTO協定の解釈の原則」として定着した．

---

(18) Report of the Panel, United States - Standards for Reformulated and Conventional Gasoline, WT/DS2/R, 29 January 1996, at 33, paras 6.7, 6.8.

(19) Report of the Appellate Body, United States - Standards for Reformulated and Conventional Gasoline, AB-1996-1, WT/DS2/AB/R, 29 April 1996, at 15-16. なお，清水・前掲注(17) 11頁.

(20) Report of the Panel, Japan - Taxes on Alcoholic Beverages, WT/DS8/R, WT/DS10/R, WT/DS11/R, 11 July 1996, at 33f., para 6.8.

(21) Report of the Appellate Body, Japan - Taxes on Alcoholic Beverages, WT/DS8/AB/R; WT/DS10/AB/R; WT/DS11/AB/R, 4 October 1996, at 9. なお，清水・前掲注(17) 12頁.

(2)　「通常の意味」と辞書の意味

ウィーン条約法31条は「解釈に関する一般的な規則」であり，32条は「解釈の補足的な手段」である．この2つの条項によると，条約を解釈するときに中心となるのは，31条1項の「条約は，文脈により且つその趣旨及び目的に照らして与えられる用語の通常の意味に従い誠実に解釈するものとする.」との定めである．そして，解釈の基礎となるのは用語の「通常の意味」である．「通常の意味」とは，一体どういう意味であるか，またどういうふうに確定すべきかが明確に定められていないのだが，パネル報告書や上級委員会報告書を見ると，辞書は「通常の意味」を確定するための重要な方法であると認められる，とされている．例えば，米国の生鮮，チルド，冷凍ラム肉輸入に係るセーフガード措置事件では，以下の展開があった．即ち――

「議長，私はこの点について最後に2つの意見があります．まず，アメリカが“cause”という用語の意味を確定するために辞書を利用することについてニュージーランドから非難を受けることは，理解できません．ウィーン条約法条約31条に反映された解釈に関する国際法上の慣習的規則によると，条約は『文脈により且つその趣旨及び目的に照らして与えられる用語の通常の意味に従い誠実に解釈するものとする.』とされています．辞書の意味を参考にすることは，通常の意味を確定するために適当な方法であることは十分に確立されています.」(22)

---

(22)　“Mr. Chairman, I have two final points on this issue. First, the United States is puzzled that New Zealand criticizes it for turning to the dictionary in seeking to determine the meaning of the term ‘cause’. Under the customary rules of interpretation of public international law, reflected in Article 31 of the Vienna Convention, a treaty ‘shall be interpreted in good faith in accordance with the ordinary meaning to be given to the terms of the treaty in their context and in the light of its object and purpose.’ It is well established that reference to diction-

―パネル第二回会合でアメリカ側の陳述.

また，パネルや上級委員会が報告書の中では，似たような意見があった.

「私たちは辞書の意味に照らして，EU やいくつかの第三国の "fair" の意味についての主張を慎重に考えました.」(23)

―パネル.

「通常の意味を確定するために，パネルは，辞書の意味から用語を解釈し始めるかもしれない.」(24)

―上級委員会.

「辞書は，協定や法律文書にある用語の意味を解釈する重要な指針であって，最終的な解釈を述べたものではない.」(25)

---

ary definitions is an appropriate way to determine ordinary meaning."

Report of the Panel, United States-Safeguard Measures on Imports of Fresh, Chilled of Frozen Lamb Meat from New Zealand and Australia, WT/DS177/R；WT/DS178/R,21 December 2000, Annex 3-9, at A-450, para.41.

(23) "We have carefully considered the arguments of the European Communities and some of the third parties regarding the ordinary meaning of the word 'fair' in light of dictionary definitions."

Report of the Panel, United States-Laws, Regulations and Methodology for Calculating Dumping Margins ("Zeroing"), WT/DS294/R, 31 October 2005, at 140f, para.7.260.

(24) "In order to identify the ordinary meaning, a panel may start with the dictionary definition of the terms to be interpreted."

Report of the Appellate Body, United States -Measures Affecting the Cross-Border Supply of Gambling and Betting Service, WT/DS285/AB/R, 7 April 2005, at 56f, para.164.

(25) "Dictionaries are important guides to, not dispositive statements of, definitions of words appearing in agreements and legal documents."

Report of the Appellate Body, United States -Continued Dumping and Subsidy Offset Act of 2000, WT/DS217/AB/R; WT/DS234/AB/R, 16 January 2003, at 78 f., para.248.

──上級委員会.

以上の議論から見ると，ウィーン条約法条約31条に定められている「通常の意味」が明確に定義されていないにもかかわらず，辞書の意味は当事国やパネル，上級委員会にとって，紛争事件において「通常の意味」を確定するための重要な方法であるからということで，条約を解釈するときに利用されるようになったことが知られる(26).

1996年，上級委員会は米国－ガソリン基準事件でThe New Shorter Oxford English Dictionary on Historical Principles (1993) を利用して，初めて辞書の利用をWTO紛争処理手続きに導入した(27). その後辞書は，パネル報告書であっても，上級委員会報告書であっても，頻繁に利用されるようになった. WTO紛争処理の専門家であるPetersmannは，辞書の利用に対して，「上級委員会の知恵のおかげで，1995年以来，オックスフォード英語辞典がほとんどの上級委員会の報告に利用され，WTO法の解釈のための1つの重要な方法となっている」(28)と称賛した.

(26) Lo, supra note1, at 431.

(27) Report of the Appellate Body, supra note 25, at 20, notes 40, 41.

(28) "Thanks to the wisdom of the Appellate Body of the [WTO], the Oxford English Dictionary has been cited in almost every appellate report since 1995 and is emerging as one of the leading sources for the interpretation of WTO law." Ernst-Ulrich Petersmann, Tribute: On the Constitution of John Jackson, 20 Mich. J. Int'l L. (1999), at 149.

第Ⅱ章　パネル報告書における辞書の「利用」

1　辞書の利用の全体的状況

次の**表1**と**図1**で，2010年まで紛争事件のパネル報告書における辞書の利用の全体の状況が分かる．

表1　各年次に採択されたパネル報告書数，辞書を利用した報告書数，利用された辞書の種類数と報告書に利用された辞書の種類の平均値(1)

年次	採択されたパネル報告書数	辞書を利用した報告書数	利用された辞書の種類数	報告書に利用された辞書種類の平均値（小数点以下1桁まで）
1996	2	1	3	3
1997	5	2	2	1
1998	11	8	10	1.3
1999	10	9	31	3.4
2000	15	14	47	3.4
2001	13	13	61	4.7

(1)　パネル報告書が採択された年次を基準とする．合併ケースの場合，1件として計算する．各報告書に利用された辞書の種類の数を合算するが，但し書名と版数がはっきり示されていない辞書は不算入とする．このため，例えばメキシコの電気通信サービスに対する措置事件では，アメリカが辞書を引用したが，パネルの報告書の中に，引用された辞書の書名と版数がはっきり示されていないから，その扱いも不算入となる．なお，本書巻末資料1，3参照．

2002	14	12	54	4.5
2003	6	6	23	3.8
2004	8	8	43	5.4
2005	13	13	55	4.2
2006	4	4	22	5.5
2007	6	5	11	2.2
2008	8	7	36	5.1
2009	4	4	19	4.8
2010	5	4	43	10.8

図1　各年次に採択されたパネル報告書数，辞書を利用した報告書数と報告書に利用された辞書の種類の平均値

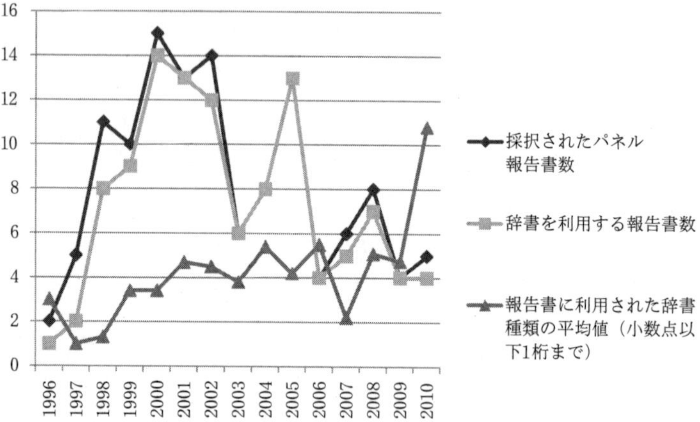

図1で，辞書を利用した報告書数を表す線と採択されたパネル報告書数を表す線はほぼ重なっている．また，1999年から，ほとんどのパネル紛争事件の報告書の中で辞書が利用された．2003年には採択されたパネル報告書の数が急落したが，報告書の中で辞書が利用されることは変わらなかった．また，報告書に利用された辞書

の種類数を表す線は下がることもあるが，全体として見ると上昇している．2010年に急な上昇があるが，その原因は，2010年に採択された中国の出版物及び音響映像製品の貿易権及び流通サービスに関する措置事件とEUによるIT製品の関税上の取扱事件のパネル報告書の中で，多数の辞書が利用されたことにある．

2　2つの事件の報告書における辞書の利用

Lo教授は，前説の論文の中で，2010年1月に採択された中国の出版物及び音響映像製品の貿易権及び流通サービスに関する措置事件のパネル報告書(2)における辞書の利用について表を示した(3)．だが，この表は報告書の一部分だけについてのものであった．そこで，各当事国やパネルがこの事件の議論において行った辞書の利用の全体像を把握するため，私は以下の表を作り，報告書中での辞書の利用箇所全てを挙げることとした．

表2　中国の出版物及び音響映像製品の貿易権及び流通サービスに関する措置事件のパネル報告書（2009年）における辞書の利用

利用された辞書	用語	出所
●New Shorter Oxford English Dictionary, L. Brown (ed.) (Clarendon Press 1993)	distribution without prejudice to unify recording distributor	Para.5.42 Para.5.7 Para.7.50 Para.7.1155 Para.7.1458

(2)　Report of the Panel, China-Measures Affecting Trading Rights and Distribution Services for Certain Publications and Audiovisual Entertainment Products, WT/DS363/R, 12 August 2009.

(3)　Lo, supra note1, at 439f.

●Shorter Oxford English Dictionary, 5th ed. (Clarendon Press 2002)	without prejudice to regulate import related to distribution video software entertainment	Para.7.253 Para.7.256 Para.7.257 Para.7.268 Para.7.1178 Para.7.1327 Para.7.1328 Para.7.1328
●Black's Law Dictionary, 7th ed., B.A. Garner (ed.) (West Group 1999)	without prejudice to discretionary	Para.7.253 Para.7.324
●American Heritage Dictionary, 4th ed. (Houghton Mifflin 2000), available at http://www.bartleby.com/61/	including include distribution	Para.7.294 Para.7.294 Para.7.1162
●Oxford English Dictionary Online available at http://dictionary.oed.com/entrance.dtl	audiovisual subscription digital product record video distribution	Para.7.340 Para.7.965 Para.7.1151 Para.7.1188 Para.7.1212 Para.7.1325 Para.7.1457
●The New Century Chinese English Dictionary	电影	Para.7.531
●Shorter Oxford English Dictionary, 6th ed. (Clarendon Press 2007)	distribution recording commodity	Para.7.1162 Para.7.1173 Para.7.1179
●Businessdictionary.com	distribution	Para.7.1180
●The Monash Marketing Dictionary www.buesco.monash.edu.au/mkt/dictionary	distribution channel	Para.7.1180
●Random House Unabridged Dictionary, (Random House 1997) available at http://dictionary.infoplease.com/distribution	distribution	Para.7.1457

●Webster's New Encyclopedic Dictionary, (Black Dog & Leventhal 1993)	distribution	Para.7.1457
●BNET Business Dictionary available at http://dictionary.bnet.com/definition/Distribution+Channel.html	distribution channel	Para.7.1458

但し，中国の出版物及び音響映像製品の貿易権及び流通サービスに関する措置事件のパネル報告書は，辞書が最も多く利用された報告書，ではない．下の表3にEUによるIT製品の関税上の取扱事件のパネル報告書(4)において利用された辞書を，まとめておく．

表3　EUによるIT製品の関税上の取扱事件のパネル報告書で利用された辞書

● Dictionary of Business Terms (3rd ed.)
● Foldoc, Free Online Dictionary of Computing, http://foldoc.org/index.cgi?query=set+top+box
● IEEE Standard Dictionary of Electrical and Electronics Terms (6th ed. 1996)
● ITV Dictionary, http://www.itvdictionary.com
● Le nouveau Petit Robert (2000)
● McGraw-Hill Dictionary of Scientific and Technical Terms, 1993
● McGraw-Hill Dictionary of Scientific and Technical Terms, 1994
● McGraw-Hill Dictionary of Scientific and Technical Terms, 2003
● Merriam-Webster online Dictionary
● Microsoft Computer Dictionary (5th ed., 2002)
● New Shorter Oxford English Dictionary, 1993 (4th edition)
● New Shorter Oxford English Dictionary, fifth edition, 2002
● New Shorter Oxford English Dictionary, fifth edition, 2003
● Newton's Telecom Dictionary (10th ed. 1996)

(4) Reports of the Panel, European Communities and its Member States Tariff Treatment of Certain Information Technology Products, WT/DS375/R; WT/DS376/R; WT/DS377/R, 16 August 2010.

- Newton's Telecom Dictionary (2004, 20th ed.)
- Newton's Telecom Dictionary (24th Ed. 2008)
- Oxford English Dictionary (2nd ed. 1989)
- Techweb On-line Dictionary，available at: http://www.techweb.com/encyclopedia/defineterm.jhtml?term=flatpaneldisplay
- The Authoritative Dictionary of IEEE Standard Terms (2000)
- The Dictionary of International Trade
- The Dictionary of Trade Policy Terms
- The Shorter Oxford Dictionary (1993)
- The Shorter Oxford Dictionary (2002)
- The Shorter Oxford Dictionary (2003)
- Webster's New Encyclopedia Dictionary (1993)
- Yourdictionary.com, http://www.yourdictionary.com/set-top-box

以上の２つの表を見ると，紛争処理手続きにおいて，いかに辞書が頻繁に利用されているかが分かるであろう．

ところが，WTOの紛争事件において，条約を解釈するときに辞書が広範に利用される一方で，辞書の利用自体も議論の争点となることがますます多くなって来ている．

次に，具体的な例を通じて，これらの問題を検討する．

3　紛争事件において多発する辞書の利用についての論争

⑴　いくつかの実例

①　中国の出版物及び音響映像製品の貿易権及び流通サービスに関する措置事件において中国が承諾した「音楽録音流通サービス」(sound recording distribution services) が「電子的な配信」(electronic distribution) 或いはインターネット音楽サービスを含むかどうかについて

●**背景**：中国は，「文化部インターネット文化管理暫定規定の実施に関する通知」，「文化部インターネット音楽発展と管理に関する若干の意見」,「文化分野における外資導入に関する若干の意見」等の政策で,「各地で外資インターネットサービス提供者が行うインターネット文化活動の許可の申請を一時的に受理しない.」「外国投資者がインターネットによる視聴プログラムサービス,ニュースサイト,出版などに携わることを禁止する.」と定めている(5).米国は,これらの産業に対する外資の参入の禁止は,外国投資者によるインターネットや移動通信網を使った録音製品の流通(distribution)に対する制限となり,中国のサービス約束表にある「音楽録音流通サービス」(sound recording distribution services)に関するGATS 16条の市場アクセス及び同17条の内国民待遇の約束に違反する,と主張した(6).

●**中国の主張**:「録音」(recording)とは記録プロセスの結果を含む実物媒体であり(7),「流通」(distribution)はShorter Oxford English Dictionary(2007年版)及びAmerican Heritage Dictionary of the English Language(2000年版)の2つの辞書によれば,「物品或いは商品」(goods, commodities)のマーケティングと供給という意味である(8).通常物品と商品は有形物であるから,中国が承諾した「音楽録音流通サービス」(sound recording distribution services)は音楽を録音した媒体,例えばCDなどのマーケティン

---

(5) 「文化部インターネット文化管理暫定規定」の実施に関する通知(2003年7月4日──「二　各地で外資インターネットサービス提供者が行うインターネット文化活動の許可の申請を一時的に受理しない.」)「文化部インターネット音楽発展と管理に関する若干意見」(2006年11月20日──「(八)──外商投資のインターネット文化経営会社の設立を禁止する.」)「外商投資禁止産業目録」(2007改定──「十,文化,体育と娯楽業　7.ニュースサイト,インターネット視聴プログラムサービス,インターネット接続サービス営業場所,インターネット文化経営」).

(6) Report of the Panel, supra note 36, at 15ff., paras.4.67-4.71.

(7) Id. at 358, paras.7.1173, 7.1174.

(8) Id. at 356, note 650.

グと供給だけに限定されていて，インターネット音楽サービス等による無形物の送信を含まない(9)．

● **米国の主張**：The New Shorter Oxford English Dictionary（1993年版）によると，「録音」（recording）は「後の再生のために視聴覚信号を記録する行為或いはプロセス」（the action or process of recording audio or video signals for subsequent reproduction）または「記録されたもの」（recorded material）(10)であり，有形物と無形物を区別しない(11)．また“distribution”の対象には，物品だけではなくサービスも含まれているから，「音楽録音流通サービス」（sound recording distribution services）は音楽を録音した有形物のマーケティングと供給のみに限定されていない(12)．

● **パネル報告**：「音楽録音流通サービス」（sound recording distribution services）は「音楽録音」（sound recording）と「流通サービス」（distribution services）の2つの部分によって構成される．「音楽録音」（sound recording）を解釈するときに重要なのは“recording”の意味である．Shorter Oxford English Dictionary（07年版）によると，「録音」（recording）の意味は「記録されたもの；記録された放送番組，公演」（recorded material; a recorded broadcast, performance.）である．“recorded material”は，中国が主張するように「録音の材料」（recording material）ではなく，「録音されたもの」（material that is recorded）と考えるべきである．“recorded material”の後についている2つの例「記録された放送番組」（recorded broadcast）と「録音された公演」（recorded performance）もこの理解を支持する．この2つの例は，録音されたもの，つまり録音の内容であり，録音を乗せる媒体ではないから，「音楽録

(9) Id. at 26, para.4.152.
(10) Id. at 354, note 649.
(11) Ibid. para. 7.1155.
(12) Id. at 355, para. 7.1156.

音」は音楽が記録された媒体だけに限定されない[13]．また「流通サービス」については，最も重要なのは「流通」の意味である．The Shorter Oxford English Dictionary（2002年版）によれば，「流通」の意味は「商業によって消費者の間に商品を分散すること　」（the dispersal of commodities among consumers affected by commerce）である．The Shorter Oxford English Dictionary（07年版）によると，「商品」（commodity）の意味は「使用できるもの或いは価値があるもの，特に，取引の対象となるもの，原材料又は農産品」（[A] thing of use or value; spec. a thing that is an object of trade, esp. a raw material or agricultural crop）または「取引或いは利用の対象となるもの」（a thing one deals in or makes use of）である．「商品」は伝統的には有形物であることが多かったが，現代技術の発展とともに，より多くの無形物も「商品」の範囲に入ってきた．また，オンライン辞書 Businessdictionary.com によると，“distribution” の意味は「配給ルートを通じた物品とサービスの出所からの移動」（movement of goods and services from the source through the distribution channel）である．「配給ルート」の意味は，The Monash Marketing Dictionary によると，「物品とサービスが生産者から最終消費者へ移動する際に通るルート」（the path or route taken by goods and services as they move from producer to final consumer）である．以上の解釈によれば，「流通」の対象は有形物だけでなく，無形物も含むはずである．したがって，「音楽録音流通サービス」の通常の意味は，録音の媒体だけではなく，インターネットなどの電子的な録音の流通も含むべきである[14]．

●**中国側上訴意見書**：American Heritage Dictionary of the English Language（2000年版）によれば，「録音」（recording）の意味

⒀　Id. at 358, paras. 7.1173-7.1176.

⒁　Id. at 358f, paras. 7.1177-7.1181.

は「音声と映像が記録されたもの」(something on which sound or visual images have been recorded) である(15). この定義は「録音」が「記録プロセスの結果を収容する媒体」(the carrier that contains the result of a recording process) であることをはっきり示している. 2つの異なる辞書の定義が同時に存在していることは, 辞書の意味だけで「音楽録音流通サービス」という用語の意味が判断できないということを証明した. パネルはごく一部の辞書だけによって結論を下すべきではなく, 文脈により且つGATSの趣旨及び目的に照らして判断すべきである(16).

② 米国の2000年継続ダンピング・補助金相殺法事件(17)において, 米国のバード修正条項はダンピング防止協定18.1条または補助金協定32.1条におけるダンピングまたは補助金に「対する」(against) 措置であるかどうかについて

●**関連する条項：**ダンピング防止協定18.1条

「他の加盟国からのダンピング輸出**に対する**いかなる措置も, この協定により解釈される1994年のガットの規定による場合を除くほか, とることができない.」(18)(AD Agreement 18.1: No specific action *against* dumping of exports from another Member can be taken except in accordance with the provisions of GATT 1994, as interpreted by this Agreement.)

●**同上：**補助金協定32.1条

---

(15) Report of the Appellate Body, China-Measures Affecting Trading Rights and Distribution Services for Certain Publications and Audiovisual Entertainment Products, WT/DS363/AB/R, 21 December 2009, at 18, para.39.

(16) Id. at 18f., paras.38-40.

(17) Report of the Panel, United States -Continued Dumping and Subsidy Offset Act of 2000, WT/DS217/R ; WT/DS234/R, 16 September 2002.

(18) 条約邦訳は, 小寺＝中川編・前掲第Ⅰ章注(15) 54頁.

「他の加盟国の補助金**に対する**いかなる措置も，この協定により解釈される1994年のガットの規定による場合を除くほか，とることができない.」(19)（SCM Agreement : 32.1: No specific action *against* a subsidy of another Member can be taken except in accordance with the provisions of GATT 1994, as interpreted by this Agreement.）

● **米国の主張：**The New Shorter Oxford English Dictionary（1993年版）によると，“against” の意味は「……に敵対して或いは積極的に反対して」（in hostility or active opposition to），「……と接触する」（into contact with）である．つまり，「他の国のダンピングまたは補助金に対する特定の措置」であるためには，「ダンピングまた補助金に敵対して，ダンピングまた補助金と接触する」必要がある（the specific action must be in “hostile opposition to” dumping/subsidization and must “come into contact with” dumping/subsidization）．輸入された商品或いは輸入者にとって負担となる特定の措置は，「他の国のダンピングまた補助金に対する特定の措置」である．ところが，バード修正条項は輸入商品或いは輸入者に負担や責任を課さないから，「他の国のダンピングまた補助金に対する特定の措置」に当たらない(20)．

● **ECとオーストラリアの主張：**“against” の意味は，同じ The New Shorter Oxford English Dictionary（1993年版）において，米国が主張した意味のほかに，「……と競争する」（in competition with），「……に損害を与える」（to the disadvantage of），「……に抵抗する」（in resistance to），「……から保護される」（as protection from）等の意味もある．つまり，アメリカが言ったように直接に輸入商品或いは輸入者にとって負担となる特定の措置のみが「他の国

(19)　条約邦訳は，小寺＝中川編・前掲第Ⅰ章注(15) 74頁．

(20)　Report of the Panel, supra note 51, at 53, para.4.243.

のダンピングまた補助金に対する特定の措置」になるのではなく，ダンピング或いは補助された輸入と競争している国内生産者にある有利な条件を与えて彼らを保護する行為も，「他の国のダンピングまた補助金に対する特定の行為」として認定すべきである[21]．

●**日本とチリの主張**：英語版と等しく権威を有しているスペイン語版の協定の中で，“against” と対応するのは “contra” である．El Diccionario de la Real Academia Española 辞書における “contra” の解釈によると，負担と義務を課す或いは輸入製品と輸入者と接触するという特定の意味がない．また，フランス語の協定の用語から見ても，米国の主張は成立しない[22]．

●**韓国の主張**：米国の主張の根拠となる “against” の「……と接触する」（into contact with）という意味は，同じ The New Shorter Oxford English Dictionary（93 年版）によると，一般的に物理的接触の意味であるから，WTO 協定には適用できない．辞書によると “against” の定義の中で一番前の定義は「……に反対する行動或いは動作」（[o]f motion or action in opposition）である．非物理的プロセスに適用する場合，“against” の最も適当な意味は「……に反対する」（in opposition）であるはずだ[23]．

●**パネル報告**：紛争当事国が主張した “against” の意味を総合的に考慮すると，“against” のすべての意味の共通点は一種の「不利な影響」（adverse bearing）の意味を持っていることである[24]．オックスフォード英語オンライン辞書によれば，“against” は「動作を表す数多くの名詞・動詞と共に用いられ，その動作の不利な影響を表す」（expressing the adverse bearing of many verbs and nouns of

---

(21) Id. at 72 & 159, para.4.364 & para.4.855.

(22) Id. at 181, para 4.989.

(23) Id. at 194, para4.1066 & para.4.1068.

(24) Id. at 301, note 271.

action)[25]．この影響は，直接な影響に限定されない[26]．

③ 米国のカナダからの軟材に対する相殺関税決定事件[27]におけるカナダの立木伐採権（Provincial Stumpage）が補助金協定1.1(a)(1)(iii)にいう政府が提供した「物品」(goods) に当たるか否かについて

補助金及び相殺措置に関する協定の１条【補助金の定義】の1.1は以下のようで定めている．

「この協定の適用上，次の(a)の(1)又は(2)のいずれか及び(b)の条件が満たされる場合には，補助金は，存在するものとみなす．

(iii)政府が一般的な社会資本以外の物品若しくは役務を提供し又は物品を購入すること．」[28]

(For the purpose of this agreement, a subsidy shall be deemed to exist if:

(a)(1) there is a financial contribution by a government or any public body within the territory of a member (referred to in this agreement as “government”), i.e. where:

(iii) a government provides *goods* or services other than general infrastructure, or purchases goods；)

●**カナダの主張：**ブラック法律辞典によれば「物品」(goods) は，有形または移動できる金銭以外の動産（“tangible or movable personal property, other than money”）という意味である．アメリカがカナダ政府から提供されたと認定したものが立木であれ，立木の伐

(25) Ibid. note 270.

(26) Id. at 306, para7.33.

(27) Report of the Panel, United States – Final Countervailing Duty Determination with Respect to Certain Softwood Lumber from Canada, WT/DS257/R, 29 August 2003.

(28) 条約邦訳は，小寺＝中川・前掲第Ｉ章注(15) 56 頁．

採権であれ，“goods”にはならない．もしアメリカが，カナダ政府が提供したのは立木を伐採する権利であると認定すれば，その権利は，無形の権利である．無形の権利によって物品を有することができても，或いは権利者の目的がこの権利によって物品を生産することであっても，無形の権利は物品だと考えてはならない．もしアメリカが，カナダが提供したのは立木自身であると認定するならば，立木は森林で生長していて，移動できない（immovable）から，物品にもならない[29]．

●**米国の主張：**同じ辞書における「物品」（goods）のもう1つの意味は，「不動産から分離されるもの」（identified thing to be severed from real property）であるから，今回紛争になった立木も含まれているはずである[30]．

●**パネル報告：**提供されたのが立木の伐採権であれ，立木自身であれ，その結果は，資格を有する伐採業者に立木を提供することである[31]．オックスフォード英語辞書（The New Shorter Oxford Dictionary 1993）によれば，「物品」（goods）の意味は「売買できる商品，品物，製品」（saleable commodities, merchandise, wares）である．ブラック法律辞典によれば，「物品」は──「1．有形または移動できる金銭以外の動産；特に，取引の対象となる製品〈物品とサービス〉．物品の販売はUCC2条によって規律される．2．有形物であるかどうにかかわらず，価値があるもの〈ソーシャルグッズの重要性は社会によって様々である〉という意味である．」（1. Tangible or movable personal property other than money; esp. articles of trade or items of merchandise <goods and services>. The sale of goods is governed by Article 2 of the UCC. 2. Things that have value, whether tangible or not <the importance of social goods varies

(29) Report of the Panel, supra note 61, at 72, para.7.3.

(30) Id. at 73, para.7.7.

(31) Id. at 77, para.7.18.

from society to society>.）とされており，またUCC§2-102(a)(24).においては，「物品」についての定義は非常に広範であり，まだ生まれていない動物の子供，生長中の農産物及びその他不動産から分離されたもの（the unborn young of animals, growing crops, and other identified things to be severed from real property）も含む．以上の定義によると，「物品」（goods）の概念は広範であり，立木（standing timber）も含むべきである[32]．

④ 米国の国境を越えた賭博サービス規制措置事件[33]における米国の自由化約束表において除外される「スポーティング」（sporting）には賭博が含まれるかどうかについて

● **米国の主張**：The New Shorter Oxford English Dictionary（1993版）によると，「スポーティング」（sporting）の意味は「運動の動作，運動への参加，娯楽，レクエーション」（[t]he action of sport, “as well as” participation in sport; amusement; recreation）及び「運動に興味，関心がある……単に金銭的な動機でスポーツに関心がある人……今特に賭博と関連する或いは賭博に興味がある」（[i]nterested in or concerned in sport; ... a person interested in sport from purely mercenary motives ... [n]ow esp[ecially] pertaining to or interested in betting or gambling）である．またThe Merriam-Webster's Collegiate Dictionary（2001）においては，「スポーティング」は「運動の，運動に関わる，運動に使われる，或いは運動に適している」（of, relating to, used, or suitable for sport）或いは「放蕩，特に賭博の，或いはそれらに関連する」（of or relating to dissipation and ESP [ecially] gambling）の意味であるから，「賭博」を

(32)　Id. at 78, para. 7.23 & 7.24.

(33)　Report of the Panel, United States -Measures Affecting the Cross-Border Supply of Gambling and Betting Service, WT/DS285/R, 10 November 2004.

含むはずである[34].

● **EU（第三国）の主張**：The Webster's New World Dictionary of American English の中で,「スポーティング」は以下のように解釈されている[35].

「スポーティング［形］

1　スポーツの，スポーツに関するまたスポーツ用の，或いは運動競技，等々.

2　スポーツ，運動競技が好きな，また参加する，等々.

3　スポーツマンらしい，公正な.

*4　賭博で特徴づけられるゲーム，レースなどが好きな，また関する.

5　［生物］変異する傾向がある.

*アメリカニズム」

（Sporting, *adj*.

1　of, having to do with, or for sports, or athletic games, etc.

2　interested in or taking part in sports, or athletic games, etc.

3　sportsmanlike; fair

*4　interested in or having to do with games, races, etc. characterized by gambling or betting

5　*Biol*. inclined to mutate –

*Americanism ）

「スポーティング」の「賭博」（gambling）と関わる定義は，辞書によると「アメリカニズム」な語法であるから，通常の定義ではないことが明らかである．そのため，アメリカが主張したこの定義がウィーン条約法条約による「通常の意味」に当たるかどうかについて，疑問がある．また，サービスの方面に用いられる場合の「ス

(34)　Id. at 22, para.3.45.

(35)　Id. at 125, para.4.22 & para.4.23.

ポーティング」の意味は，「賭博で特徴づけられるゲーム，レースなどと関係がある」（having to do with games, races, etc. characterized by gambling or betting）であっても，この定義から，「スポーティング　サービス」（sporting services）は「賭博サービス」（gambling and betting services）を含むという結論を導き出すことはできないのである．

●**アンチグアの主張**：The New Shorter Oxford Dictionary によると，「スポーティング」には動名詞と形容詞両方の用法がある．動名詞として，「運動の動作」（the action of sport）と「運動に参加すること，娯楽，レクリエーション」（participation in sport; amusement, recreation）を意味する．辞書によると，「（運動）に関係して」の意味で他の用語と一緒に使われる．これはまさに皆が思っているアメリカ約束表における「スポーティング　サービス」についての用法であろう．「スポーティング」には形容詞としても幾つかの意味があるけれども，通常「サービス」等の用語と一緒に使われないのである．その他，アメリカはパネルへの回答書の中で「スポーティング」は「他の賭博ではない運動の形態」（other [non-gambling] forms of sporting）も含むと主張したが，そうなると，アメリカが主張したのは「スポーティング」の通常の意味によることではなく，辞書にある全ての意味を含むということになる．アメリカの主張によれば，今回の場合は，「売春」（prostitution），「リスクを取ることに関連するサービス」（services relating to the taking of risks）も含まれるはずである．辞書の中でこれらの意味があるのは事実だが，1つの文献の中で使われた「スポーティング」という用語は，同時に全ての意味を有することはできないのである(36)．

●**米国の主張**：The New Shorter Oxford English Dictionary においては，「スポーティング」の「賭博」と関わる定義は「アメリ

(36)　Id. at 28, para.3.62.

カニズム」な語法であるという説明は，ないのである．また，米国は英語用語の「通常の意味」の基準となることはできないといった，条約解釈上のルールとしての禁止はないのである．それに，対象となるのはアメリカが承諾した約束表であるから，「アメリカニズム」という理由で辞書におけるその定義を排除することは，不合理である(37)．

(2) 様々な辞書

以上のいくつかの事件での各国の議論を見て，何かおかしいと思わないか．なぜ，紛争処理手続きにおいて条約を解釈するとき，辞書における語彙の定義の相違が論争の焦点になるのか．

「辞書」と言えば，権威と中立のイメージが漠然と浮かび上がるであろうが，実際はどうであろうか．ここでまず注意しなければならないのは，辞書が様々であり，そして，同じ用語に対しても異なる辞書においては異なる定義があること，である(38)．例として，ここで有名なオックスフォード英語辞典を見る．オックスフォード英語辞典（Oxford English Dictionary）といっても，実は様々な種類がある．以下の表では，紛争事件において実際に利用されたオックスフォード英語辞典（Oxford English Dictionary）を挙げた．

表4　紛争事件において実際に利用されたオックスフォード英語辞典（Oxford English Dictionary）(39)

- Concise Oxford English Dictionary (1990, 1995, 2001, 2002, 2004)
- Oxford English Dictionary Online, http://dictionary.oed.com
- Oxford English Reference Dictionary (1995)

---

(37) Id. at 29, para.3.64.

(38) Phillip A. Rubin, War of the Words: How Courts Can Use Dictionaries in accordance with Textualist Principles, Duke Law Journal, Vol. 60 (2010), at 177.

(39) **表4**は，パネルや上級委員会の報告書で利用された時の書名による．

- Oxford Standard Dictionary
- Oxford Student's Dictionary
- Shorter Oxford English Dictionary (1973, 1983, 1990, 1993, 2002, 2003, 2007)
- The Compact Edition of the Oxford English Dictionary (1971, 1985)
- The Compact Oxford English Dictionary (1971, 1987)
- The Concise Oxford Dictionary (1995, 1999, 2001)
- The Concise Oxford Dictionary of Current English (1976, 1980, 1990, 1995)
- The Concise Oxford Dictionary of the English Language
- The New Little Oxford Dictionary (1989)
- The New Oxford Dictionary of English (1998, 2001)
- The New Oxford Thesaurus of English
- The New Shorter Oxford English Dictionary (1990, 1993, 1996, 1997, 1999, 2002, 2003)
- The Oxford Encyclopedic English Dictionary (1991)
- The Oxford English Dictionary (1938, 1971, 1986, 1989)
- The Shorter Oxford English Dictionary on Historical Principles (1944)

辞書の編集は，最初に目的を明らかにした後，対象となる使用者層と予算により辞書のサイズを決めて，慎重な考慮と計画をしてから始まるものである(40)．オックスフォード大学出版局のホームページを見ると，出版された辞書は下のように分けられている(41)．

辞書の種類

❖ オックスフォード英語辞書—1150年からの英語の記録

(40) Howard Jackson, Lexicography: An Introduction (2002), at 161. 翻訳について，この本の日本語版を参照する．南出康世　石川慎一郎『英語辞書学への招待』（大修館書店，2004年）また Rubin, supra note 72, at 177をも参照．

(41) オックスフォード大学出版局のホームページ参照．アクセス：2012年1月20日．http://www.oed.com/staticfiles/oedtoday2/oxford_and_the_dictionary.pdf

- ❖ 一般参考及び学習研究のための現代英語辞典
- ❖ 子供と学生用の辞典
- ❖ 英語を外国語として勉強するための辞典
- ❖ 二言語辞典
- ❖ カナダ，オーストラリア，南アフリカなどの地域で使われる英語方言辞典

想定使用者と辞書のサイズは，当然のことながら，辞書の内容，収録語彙範囲に関する決定に影響を及ぼす(42)．ある分野の専門家のための辞書であれば，その分野の専門性の高い術語をたくさん収録するが，学習者用辞書は，当該言語の中核語彙に注意を向ける．机上版の辞書は，できるだけ法律・医学・農学・金融など各分野の語を収録しようとするが，ポケット版の辞書は専門語に充てるスペースは少ない．また，最新の口語，俗語，卑語，禁句や変種の言語の語彙を収録するかどうかも異なる．

辞書の編集者は，明確な計画を立てた後，まず見出し語リストを選定しなければならない(43)．そして，辞書の資料をどこから手に入れるかどうかを決める(44)．最後に記載事項を執筆する．今は，電子情報技術の発展に伴い，辞書を編集するとき，電子化されたテキストを大規模に集成したコンピュータ・コーパスがよく利用されている(45)．コンピュータ・コーパスによって，資料の収集，分類，検索等は効率的になるが，資料から自動的に完成辞書を作り出すことはない．辞書編集は，せんじ詰めれば「コンピュータ自動処理型」(computer-automated）の仕事ではなく，「コンピュータ支援型」(computer-aided) の仕事である(46)．

(42) Rubin, supra note 72, at 178 &183; Jackson, supra note 74, at 161f.
(43) Jackson, supra note 74, at 163.
(44) Id. at 166; Rubin, supra note 72, at 179.
(45) Jackson, supra note 74, at 29; Rubin, supra note 72, at 179.
(46) Jackson, supra note 74, at 171.

WTO のパネルや上級委員会の報告書を見ると，議論をするとき利用された辞書は様々である．オックスフォード英語辞典（Oxford English Dictionary），American Heritage Dictionary 等一般的な英語の辞書もあるが，ブラック法律辞典（Black's Law Dictionary），McGraw-Hill Dictionary of Scientific and Technical Terms, Newton's Telecom Dictionary, A Dictionary of the Flowering Plants and Ferns 等，法律や電子通信，生物など様々な専門分野の辞書もある．言語辞書もあるが，Webster's New Encyclopedic Dictionary 等の百科事典もある．英語辞書もあるが，Le Nouveau Petit Robert, The Dictionary of the Académie Française, Larousse French Dictionary, Diccionario de la Lengua Española 等の，仏・西の外国語の辞書もある．一言語の辞典もあるが Robert & Collins French-English Dictionary, Collins Spanish-English Dictionary, The New Century Chinese English Dictionary 等の二言語辞書もある．机上版の辞書もあるが，簡略版，コンサイス版の辞書もある．また紙の辞書が普通だが，最近では CD-ROM, オンライン辞書など電子版の辞書もよく使われる．米国による中国製品に対する AD・相殺関税最終措置事件においては，誰でも随時書き込むことができる Wikipedia の用語の意味さえ利用されるようになった(47)．

⑶ 異なる定義

以上述べたように，辞書は様々な影響を受けて編集されたものであるから，同じ語彙についても，異なる辞書においては異なる定義がある．例えば，既に挙げた④の事例の中で議論の対象となった "sporting" について，The Oxford English Dictionary（1989 年

(47) Report of the Panel, United States - Definitive Anti-dumping and Countervailing Duties on Certain Products from China, WT/DS379/R, 22 October 2010, at 60f., note 256.

版）の中では，下のように定義されている：

"Sporting, vbl.sb.[f. sport v.]

1. a. The action of the verb；engagement or participation in sport.

   b. An instance or occasion of this；a sport.

2. a. The action on the part of Nature of producing an abnormal form or variety; an instance or occasion of this. Obs. Cf. SPORT sb.6

   b. Irregular diffusion or deposition of pollen.

   c. The action on the part of plants, etc.,of deviating or varying from the parent stock or type by spontaneous mutation; an abnormal form or variation so produced; a sport.

3. attib. and Comb.

   a. In older usage, as sporting device, game, matter, place, time, etc.

   b. In later and mod. Use, As sporting celebrity, party, purpose; freq. in senses 'formed or undertaken for sport', 'concerned with or interested in sport', as sporting association, column, event, magazine, newspaper, page, paper, tour, and 'used in or for sport', as sporting bullet, cartridge, dog, gear, goods, gun, jacket.

   c. Special Combs., as sporting-box, a small residence for use during the sporting season...

Sporting, ppl. a.

1. a. Engaged in sport or play.

   b. Sportive; playful. Obs. rare.

   c. Of plants, etc.

2. a. Interested in, accustomed to take part in, field sports or similar amusements; spec. in phr. sporting person.

b. Esp. Sporting man; now used to denote a sportsman of an inferior type or one who is interested in sport from purely mercenary motives. Also used in other collocations referring to low gaming and betting.

c. N. Amer. Used spec. to denote a prostitute or loose woman, as sporting girl, woman. Cf. SPORTSWOMAN b.

3. a. Characterized by sport or sportsmanlike conduct; affording or producing sport. Also, of or characterized by conduct consonant with that of a sportsman or'good sport'.

b. sporting chance, a change such as is met with or taken in sport; one of an uncertain or doubtful nature. Also, an opportunity that a sportsman might consider. colloq."

これに対して，The Concise Oxford Dictionary of current English（1995年版）の中では，下のように簡単に定義されている．
"Sporting adj.
1 interested in sport (a sporting man).
2 sportsmanlike, generous (a sporting offer).
3 concerned with sport (a sporting dog; sporting news)."

また，Concise Oxford Thesaurus（2007年版）では，"sporting" の同義語と対義語について，下のように書かれている．
"Sporting adjective sportsmanlike, generous, gentlemanly, considerate; fair, just, honourable; Brit. informal decent.
-OPPOSITES dirty, unfair."

ところで，一言語辞書は歴史的な記述を主な目的とする「通時的」(diachronic; historical) 辞書と特定の時点・時期における語彙の記述を目的とする「同時的」(synchronic) 辞書とに区別される[48]．よく見られるのは前者である．有名な The New Shorter Oxford English Dictionary や，Webster's Third New International Dictionary of the English Language Unabridged，及び，Collins Concise Dictionary は，全て通時的な辞書である．

言語は文化の記号である．文化の発展に伴って変わっているのである．言語の記録者としての辞書も，継続的に新しい語彙及び語の新しい意味を収録してゆくべきものである．また，辞書自身の編集方法も，発展し続けている．そのため，辞書は，版の違いがあっても１つのものである聖書とは異なって[49]，異なる版の間で大きな差がありうる．例えば，上記の③の紛争事件の中で議論された "goods" の意味について見ると，

Black's Law Dictionary（1979 年版）の中で "goods" は──

"Goods. A term of variable content and meaning. It may include every species of personal property or it may be given a very restricted meaning.

Items of merchandise, supplies, raw materials, or finished goods. Sometimes the meaning of 'goods' is extended to include all tangible items, as in the phrase 'goods and services'."

──と定義されており，その中では「有形物」だけに言及されている．

一方，Black's Law Dictionary（2009 年版）の中では，"goods" は──

"Goods. (bef.12c)　1.Tangible or movable personal property other than money;esp., articles of trade or items of merchandise

(48)　Jeffrey L. Kirchmeier / Samuel Thumma, Scaling the Lexicon Fortress: The United States Supreme Court's Use of Dictionaries in the Twenty-First Century , Marquette Law Review, Vol. 94, 2010, at 97; Jackson, supra note 74, at 23; Rubin, supra note 72, at 187.

(49)　Jackson, supra note 74, at 21.

<goods and services>.The sale of goods is governed by Article 2 of the UCC.
2. Things that have value, whether tangible or not <the importance of social goods varies from society to society>."
――と定義されており，これによれば，「有形物」であるかどうかにかかわらず，価値があるもの全てが含まれる．このことからすれば，米国のカナダからの軟材に対する相殺関税決定事件におけるカナダの主張は，支持されないことにもなり得る．

(4)　曖昧な「通常の意味」

ウィーン条約法条約31条と32条は下のように規定する．

「第31条　解釈に関する一般的な規則

1.　条約は，文脈により且つその趣旨及び目的に照らして与えられえる用語の通常の意味に従い，誠実に解釈するものとする．
2.　条約の解釈上，文脈というときは，条約文（前文及び附属書を含む）のほかに，次のものを含める．
　(a)　条約の締結に関連してすべての当事国の間でされた条約の関係合意
　(b)　条約の締結に関連して当事国の一又は二以上が作成した文章であってこれらの当事国以外の当事国が条約の関係文書として認めたもの．
3.　文脈とともに，次のものを考慮する．
　(a)　条約の解釈又は適用につき当事国の間で後にされた合意
　(b)　条約の適用につき後に生じた慣行であって，条約の解釈についての当事国の合意を確立するもの
　(c)　当事国の間の関係において，適用される国際法の関連規則
4.　用語は，当事国がこれに特別の意味を与えることを意図していたと認められる場合には，当該特別の意味を有する．

第32条　解釈の補足的な手段

前条の規定の適用により得られた意味を確認するため又は次の場合における意味を決定するため，解釈の補足的な手段，特に条約の準備作業及び条約の締結の際の事情に依拠することができる．

(a)　前条の規定による解釈によっては意味があいまい又は不明確である場合

(b)　前条の規定による解釈により明らかに常識に反した又は不合理な結果がもたらされる場合」

ウィーン条約法条約31条と32条によると，条約を解釈するとき最も中心となるのは用語の「通常の意味」である．辞書は用語のすべての意味を並べようとする(50)．ウィーン条約法条約31条と32条を前提に，従来のWTO紛争処理の，本稿で示した顕著な傾向をあてはめると，分類された辞書の意味に基づいて用語の「通常の意味」を確定するために，条約の文脈，趣旨及び目的，当事国の間で後にされた合意，後に生じた慣行，適用される国際法の関連規則，条約の準備作業及び締結の際の事情など様々なものが参考になる，はずである(51)．また，「通常の意味」は曖昧であり，一種フィクションのような存在でもある(52)．「通常の意味」は自然なそれであり，通常の慣用に従った意味であるが(53)，いかなる意味が「通常の意味」であるかは，結局解釈者自身の判断にゆだねられることになる．パネルや上級委員会の報告書を見ると，用語の通常の意味を確定するためにまずある辞書の意味を提示して，それから文脈や条約

(50)　Report of the Appellate Body, supra note 31, at 50, para.164.

(51)　山形英郎「国際司法裁判所における条約解釈手段の展開――ヴァッテル規則からの脱却」日本国際経済法学会年報第19号（法律文化社，2010年）44頁.

(52)　坂元茂樹『条約法の理論と』（東信堂，2004年）145頁.

(53)　菊地正は「通常の意味」と実際「明瞭な意味」の混同を指摘する．菊地正「国際条約の解釈――原文に基づく方法――」名城法学（1972年12月）2巻1・2号235頁.

の趣旨及び目的を参照した後，選ばれた意味が文脈や条約の趣旨及び目的に合致すれば通常の意味であると判断する，というやり方が通常である．この判断方法は，一見「文脈により且つその趣旨及び目的に照らして与えられる用語の通常の意味に従い……解釈する」という要求に合致する．ところが，選ばれた辞書の意味が文脈や条約の趣旨及び目的に合致するのは，文脈や条約の趣旨及び目的だけによっては，選ばれた意味が「通常の意味」ではないということを証明できないからかもしれないのである．このような場合，文脈や条約の趣旨及び目的の参照は，実は飾りもののような存在であり，「通常の意味」についての判断は，完全に辞書の意味の選択にゆだねられることになってしまうのである．また，様々な辞書の異なる定義が存在していて，選択の余地はあまりにも大きいため，「常に……欲しい意味をサポートする辞書の意味を見つけることができる」[54]ことにもなる．その結果，WTO の紛争事件において，皆が皆それぞれの辞書の定義を根拠として，用語の通常の意味について議論することが多い，ということになるのである．

(54)　Lo, supra note 1, at 441, note 15.

第Ⅲ章　辞書とかかわるいくつかの問題点

1　条約締結後出版された辞書を利用できるのか

中国の出版物及び音響映像製品の貿易権及び流通サービスに関する措置事件において，中国は上訴意見書の中で「パネルは，中国のGATS 約束表での “video (...) distribution services” という用語を解釈するにあたって，中国が WTO に加入する時の辞書にある用語の意味を利用すべきである.」と主張した(1).

また，EU による IT 製品の関税上の取扱事件において，EU は，アメリカや台湾が 2002 年の The Microsoft Computer Dictionary を利用することに対して，異議を申し立てた(2). EU は，「アメリカや台湾がフラットパネルディスプレイ措置（Flat panel display devices）の意味を主張する際に利用したのは ITA 交渉が終わった 5 年後に出版された 2002 年版の The Microsoft Computer Dictionary における用語の意味であるから，交渉当時の用語の意味を反映させることはできない.」と指摘した. これに対して台湾は，「ITA 交渉前の 1993 年版においても，交渉後の 2003 年版の McGraw-Hill Dictionary of Scientific and Technical Terms においても，フラットパネルディスプレイ措置についての定義は 2002 年版の The Microsoft Computer Dictionary における意味と類似する.」と指摘した. パネルは，1993 年版の The Shorter Oxford Dictionary と Techweb On-line Dictionary における意味を調べた後，ア

(1) Report of the Appellate Body, supra note 49, at 20, para.43.
(2) Report of the Panel, supra note 38, at 153, para.7.474.

メリカと台湾の主張を支持した．

実は，パネルはこの紛争事件の中で，条約締結後出版された辞書を利用することができるかどうかという問題を，回避した．しかし，アメリカや台湾の主張を支持することによって，パネルは条約締結後に出版された辞書を利用することを黙認した，とも言える．

ここでまず，条約締結後に出版された辞書における用語の意味は，締結する時の意味と同じである「かもしれない」ことを認識すべきである．前に述べたように，辞書には「通時的」（diachronic; historical）辞書と「同時的」（synchronic）辞書の両方がある．前者は歴史的な記述を主な目的とする．例えば，The Oxford English Dictionary は1150年以降の，その簡約版の The Shorter Oxford English Dictionary は1700年以降の，英語語彙を構成している個々の語の形態と意味の誕生・消滅・変化を，記録している(3)．また，辞書の編集自体も時間がかかる(4)．ジョンソンの辞書には9年かかったが，初版の The Oxford English Dictionary は50年もかかっていた(5)．その結果，条約締結後に出版された辞書における用語の意味は，締結時の意味と同じである「かもしれない」．ところが，「言葉は発展するものである．過去において慣習的に使われていた意味を現在も継続的に有しているとは限らない場合もあろう(6)」．情報技術やインターネットの発展とともに，各文化の衝突，進化，融合も飛躍的に激しくなる．新語や古い言葉の新しい用法が一夜にして全国または全世界での流行となることも多くなった．一方，コンピュータ技術の発展によってコーパスが多く利用され，辞書の編集にかかる時間も短くなってきた．また，電子版の辞書，オンライン辞書等，新しい形式の辞書もたくさん出てきた．そして，

---

(3) Jackson, supra note 74, at 23.
(4) Rubin, supra note 72, at 186.
(5) Jackson, supra note 74, at 165.
(6) 坂元茂樹・前掲第Ⅱ章注(52)148頁．

ここで注意すべきなのは，既に言及した中国の出版物及び音響映像製品の貿易権及び流通サービスに関する措置事件とEUによるIT製品の関税上の取扱事件で議論の対象とされたのが電子製品方面の用語の定義だということである．この方面は近年最も速く発展してきた分野の1つとも言える．そのため，条約締結前後に出版された辞書における用語の意味が異なっている可能性も大きいのである．また，台湾がEUによるIT製品の関税上の取扱事件において，条約締結前後に出版された辞書における用語の意味は一致していると主張したが，そうであればなぜ直接条約出版前の辞書の意味を利用しなかったのか，という疑問も生ずる．

最近では，紛争事件においてオンライン辞書を利用することが急増した．下の表では，2011年2月までのWTO紛争処理手続きにおいて利用されたオンライン辞書を示す．

表5　紛争事件において利用されたオンライン辞書(7)

- A Dictionary of Accounting, (Oxford: University Press, 1999), www.xrefer.com
- Accurate and Reliable Dictionary online, http://ardictionary.com
- BNET Business Dictionary, http://dictionary.bnet.com/definition/Distribution+Channel.html
- Businessdictionary.com
- Chambers Online Reference, http://.chambersharrap.co.uk/chambers/chref/chref.py/main
- Diccionario de la Lengua Española Real Academia de Madrid, www.rae.es
- Dictionary online, http://www.thefreedictionary.com
- Encarta World English Dictionary, http://encarta.msn.com/dictionary_/sporting.html, 2004.
- Foldoc, Free Online Dictionary of Computing, http://foldoc.org/index.cgi?query=set+top+box

(7)　2011年2月までに採択されたパネル報告書と上級委員会報告書より，表5を作成した．

- Harcourt, Academic Dictionary of Science and Technology, http://www.harcourt.com/dictionary/browse
- Http://www.biology-online.org/dictionary.asp
- Http://www.yourdictionary.com/set-top-box
- ITV Dictionary, http://www.itvdictionary.com
- Merriam Webster Online Dictionary, http://www.webster.com/cgi-bin/dictionary. 2003
- Merriam-Webster's Collegiate Dictionary, http://www.m-w.com
- Oxford English Dictionary, http://dictionary.oed.com
- Random House Unabridged Dictionary, (Random House 1997), http://dictionary.infoplease.com/distribution
- Spanish Dict online, http://www.spanishdict.com/translate/perteneciente
- Techweb On-line Dictionary, http://www.techweb.com/encyclopedia/defineterm.jhtml?term=flatpaneldisplay
- The American Heritage Dictionary, http://www.bartleby.com
- The Dictionary of the Académie Française (online version)
- Trésor de la Langue Francaise, dictionary published by the CNRS (National Center for Scientific Research), http://atilf.atilf.fr/tlf.htm
- Wikipedia
- www.fishbase.org

これらのオンライン辞書は随時編集されており，用語の最新の意味を反映することができる一方，意味を定義された時間も不明確になる．したがって，これらの辞書によって条約が締結された時の用語の意味を知ることも困難になる．また，Wikipedia のような誰でも随時書き込むことができる開放型辞書に対しては，その適格性も問うべきであろう．

2　数多くの「簡単」な語について辞書の利用

(1)　パネルの報告書の中で辞書を利用する用語

下の**表6**と**表7**を通じて，2010年までの各年次に採択されたパネル報告書の中で，いくつの用語について，また，具体的に何の用語について辞書が利用されたのかを示した．

表6　各年次に採択されたパネル報告書の中で辞書を利用した報告書数，辞書の意味を利用された用語数と報告書に辞書の意味を利用された用語数の平均値(8)

年次	辞書を利用した報告書数	辞書の意味を利用された用語数	報告書に辞書の意味を利用された用語数の平均値（小数点以下1桁まで）
1996	1	2	2
1997	2	2	1
1998	8	13	1.6
1999	9	50	5.6
2000	14	86	6.1
2001	13	107	8.2
2002	12	82	6.8
2003	6	89	14.8
2004	8	100	12.5
2005	13	117	9
2006	4	78	19.5
2007	5	24	4.8

(8)　年次はパネル報告書が採択された年次を基準とする．合併の場合，1件として計算する．各報告書において辞書の意味を利用された用語の数を合算する．

2008	7	72	10.3
2009	4	45	11.3
2010	4	61	15.3

表7　各年次に採択されたパネル報告書の中で辞書の意味を利用された用語一覧(9)

年次	辞書の意味を利用された用語
1996	**so as; so as to**
1997	good faith
1998	**base**; directory provision; displace; effect; exclusive; likelihood; measure; **potential; probability; serious**
1999	advantage; anticipate; application; **available; benefit;** burden of proof; case; circumvent; conditioned; confer; consume; consumer; contingent; distillation; entrust; evidence; expectation; field; finance; **gradually;** grant; mandate; mandated; **material;** nectarine; **obtain; payment;** payments-in-kind; phase out; **potential;** proceeding; proceedings; **provide;** provision; remunerate; **represents**; restriction; statement; substantially; thereupon; **trade; variety;** warranted
2000	a separate legal entity of a corporation; **activity; acts; advantage;** agent; **all;** application; arm's length transaction; **available;** benefit; branch; **case; certain; clarity; commence; condition;** contingent; decision; define; delay; **demonstrate; determination; determine;** discretion; discrimination; **due;** economic; enjoyment; ensure; enterprise; entity; **essential;** evidence; exploit; fair market value; grant; **immediately; include;** increase; independence; instrument; interests; interlocutory; investigation; **law**; legislative history; legitimate; limited; mandatory; marketing; **may; normal;** offset; prejudice; prescribe; prescriptive; processes; provide; provision; **reasonable;** refer; requirements; revenue; **rule;** sanctity; **shall; should; special;** statement; subject matter; subordinate; to deter; unconditional; undertake; unreasonable; unwarranted

(9)　用語が重複した場合，1つとして記載する．

2001	**actual;** adverse; adverse inference rule; allegation; asbestos; **average; basis; believe; between;** body; **cause**; characteristic; charge; circumspection; **comparable; competitive; condition**; conjecture; **consider; consideration**; constructive; cooperate; **determination; determine; direct; directs**; discrimination; **document**; eligible; emergency measures; endeavor; entrust; **essential**; evaluate; evaluation; evidence; examination; explore; **fact; favourable; immediately**; imminent; impact; impartial; **include; including**; inform; justifiable; **least**; link; **may; method; necessary**; notify; objective; ordinary course of business; output; positive; **possibility**; primary; procedure; **process; produce**; producer; product; production; **reasonable**; redress; remain; remedy; representative; restriction; **result**; retaliation; sanction; seeking; serious damage; **significant; special; standard; such as; sufficient**; suspect; term; terms of sale; to carry out; to demonstrate; to discern; to focus; to seek; type; unbiased; unexpected; unforeseen; uniform; weighted; **whether; whole**; withhold; **would**; yam count
2002	affidavit; **against; all;** anticipated; appropriately; as a basis; as is; **available; benefit; best; bring;** category; **clear;** counteract; derogate; **determine; economic;** el titular; evaluation; explore; explored; fair; fix; **good; goods; ground;** having a bearing on; imminent; importation; in particular; in relation to; in respect of; inappropriate; ineffective; information; inherent; is being imported; **known;** label; le titulaire; letter of awareness; letter of comfort; name; necessary; offset; **on;** operationalize; **ordinary; other;** owner; performance; prevailing; **proper; provide; provides; reasonable;** relevant; remedy; requirement; res judicata; response; sardines; **should; similar;** specify; subject matter; substantiate; take into account; tariff quota; telle quelle; timber; to publish; to pursue; to the best of one's ability; undue; **use;** variable import levy; variable levies; verifiable; verification; verify; withhold
2003	**actual;** adjustment; **appropriate;**as instrument; causal; **cause;** circumventing; circumvention; coincide; **comparable; compare; competition; condition;** context; create; **determine; development;** disrupt; disruptive; disrupts; distorting; distortion; drill; emergency; **essential;** estoppel; evaluate; evidence; explore; extent; facilitar; facilitate; **fact;** fitting; **have;** having a bearing on; impartial; **important;** increase; increased;

	instrument; investigate; **like;** majeur; **major;** major part; **majority; material; nature;**negligible; **objective;** participate; prevent; **product;promptly; proper;** proportion; provide; rate; **reason; reasonable;** regard; remedy; res judicata; restrictive; **result;** satisfied; simultaneous; simultaneously; source; statement; strict; subjective; suitable; **that;** to pursue; transship; unduly; uniform; **used;** warrant; **when; whether**
2004	adequate; administrative; advantage; affirmative defence; **also; any;** appropriate; basis; care; characteristic; circumstance; **close; commercial; competitive; conditional; right; consider;** continuation; de facto; **determination; determine;** discriminate; discriminatory tariff; distribution; ensure; exception; expeditious; **fair;** G&A; **general;** general costs; generaliser; generalize; **good; goods;** guideline; identify; imminent; impartial; **in relation to;** industry; initiative; interconnect; interconnection; irrefutable; licence; **likely; limited;** link; major proportion; mutatis mutandis; necessary; non-discriminatory; non-discriminatory tariff; notwithstanding; offset; **own;** pertain; positive right; practices; prevailing; **probable;** procedural; procedure; property; **provides; rational; reasonable;** recurrence; resemble; review; **shall; special;** special exception; statutory exception; telecommunications; facilities; **the;** timely; to inform; to initiate; to orient; transmission facility; unconditional; unconditionally; undertake; uniform; **unless; use;** vulnerable; **whole; will**
2005	**action; against; any;** arbitrary; base; best; body; chilled; circumvent; commitments; commodity; concern; **consider; cost; cover;** cure; **decide;** depression; designate; **determination; determine;** detriment; **direct;** dried; entertainment; entrust; estoppel by; exempt; express; form; freeze; fresh; frozen; gamble; gambling; grant; illustrative; in brine; inadequate; **include; industry; interest;** investigate; investigator; **known; likely;** limitations; link; long-term; losses; market; market access; matters; **may;** moral; **necessary;** non liquet; **none;** notwithstanding; numerical; offset; **on;** operate; operating; order; **original;** output; practice; prejudice; premiums; preserve; prevent; price; proceeding; process; product; programme; public; public body; quota; **reasonable;** recreation; recreational; redress; related; relationship; rely; restriction; salted; seeking; **separate; serious;**

	share; **significant; silence;** smoked; specific; sporting; substantial; suppress; to bet; to investigate; to prepare ; to salt; to seek; unjustifiable; **use**
2006	acrylate; additives; administer; administration; allergen; aplicar; application; appliquer; apply; at issue; audit; biodiversity; brief; classification; **complete;** compliance; comply; contaminant; damage; de facto; delay; discretion; disease; entry; evaluate; execute; exempt; existence; failure; fair; fauna; **food; general;** govern; **independent;** international agreement; investigation; **laws;** manner; microbial toxin; moratorium; mycotoxin; mycotoxins; ordinance; organism; penalties; pertaining to; pest; phase; potential; procedure; procedure; process; record-keeping; regulations; release; review; **secure; shall; standard;** substance; summary; suspension; take account of ; **the;** to arise from; toxin; transparency; transparent; trophic; undertake; **undue;** uniform; uniformity; valuation; weeds
2007	accumulate; accumulation; administrative; arbitrary; **comparison;** discretionary; examine; **fair;** funds; interested; interested parties; invest; investigation; justifiable; licence; **method;** phase; procedure; **rational;** requirement; rice; to exempt; transfer; unjustifiable
2008	**actual; adequate; appropriate;** arise; charge; commence ; complaint; cost; crear; creation; critical; critical mass; critical size; deliberation; determine; due; duty; endocrine; system; endocrinology; endogenous; epidemiology; equal in; force; equality; equivalent; establish; establishment; **fact; formally; good faith; insufficient; invite; measure; necessary;** obiter dictum; **or; ordinary; possibility; potential; produce; producer; producers; production; reasonable;** reasonableness; restraint; **science; scientific;** suspected; **to;** typically; verifiable
2009	anti-circumvention; as presented; authority; avoid; **car;** circumvent; circumvention; commercial; consignment; customs; duties; disposal; dispose; **during;** exceptional; existence; fair; freedom; guarantee; importation; internal taxes; investigation; kit; levy; motor; **on; ordinary; part; payment; price; principles;** restriction; scale; screwdrive operations; **shall; simple;** SKD; split; tax avoidance; tax evasion; **the;** transit; valuation; **value; vehicle; whole**

2010	an electronic display; andiovisual; approval; approving; arbitrary; audio; authorization; **ban;** bring about; classify; commodity; **complete;** consumer; devices; digital; discretionary; display; distribution; distribution channel; distributor; elaborate; entertainment; flat panel display devices; **for;** import; importation; **include; including;** indication; **intermediate;** involved; justifiable; LCD display; **material; modern;** mutatis mutandis; negligible; output units; panel; photocopying; printer; procedure; product; publish; record; recorded material; recording; **regulate; related to;** requirement; set top box; software; subscription; undertake; uniform; unity; unjustifiable; video; visual; **without;** prejudice; xerography; 电影

表7を見て，多くの人が意外に思われるのではないだろうか．辞書を引く用語は，皆が普段から慣れている語彙ばかりである．それに加え，“the”，“may”，“on”，“without”，“will”，“should”，“shall”，“for”，“from”，“any” などの助動詞，冠詞，前置詞についてさえ，辞書の意味が利用された．ところが，これらの用語自体の意味はあまりにも広すぎるし，その意味は文法や文脈によって確定されることが多い(10)．また，当事国やパネル，上級委員会が調べたのは Oxford English Dictionary，Merriam-Webster's Dictionary 等通常の辞書であり，条約用語を定義するための専門的な辞書ではない．つまり，これらの辞書によって，これらの用語に条約における特別な意味や用法を与えることは，できないはずなのである(11)．そうであれば，WTO のパネルや上級委員会は，一体何のために，これらの用語について辞書の意味を利用するのであろうか．

そこで，次に，まず前置詞 “on” を例として，パネルがいくつか

(10) 「専門語や固有名詞などは一つの意味しか持っていないことが多いが，日常語では，一つの語が二つ以上の意味を持っているのがむしろ普通である．しかも，使用頻度の高い語ほど多くの意味を持っている傾向がある．……多義語が文中で用いられたとき，その語彙を決定するのは文脈あるいは場面である．」佐藤弘『英語辞書の実際』（八潮出版社，1982）33 頁．

(11) 佐藤弘・前掲注(10)33 頁．

の紛争事件でどのように辞書の意味を利用して“on”の意味を解釈したかを見た後，再びこの問題について議論をすることとする.

(2)　紛争事件で問題となった“on”についての解釈

“on”は皆が普段から慣れている前置詞であるが，いくつかの紛争事件において，特にその意味について議論がなされた.

①　インドの自動車部門における貿易と投資に係る措置事件[12]

まず，インドの自動車部門における貿易と投資に係る措置事件において，パネルがGATT11条1項に規律するのは国境措置（border measures）だけであるか否かについていかなる分析をしたか，を見る.

1997年，インド商務省は，自動車部品輸入許可政策に関する公示60号を採択した[13]．この公示は，自動車の組立キットを輸入しようとする乗用車製造業者に外国貿易総局と了解覚書を締結することを要求するものであった．乗用車製造業者に対しては，了解覚書の中では，現地化要件と「各乗用車製造業者は了解覚書の有効期間以内に組立キットの輸入額と完成車及び自動車部品の輸出額を均衡させなければならない」という貿易収支均衡要件を課すことになった[14]．EUとアメリカは，インドの政策がGATT3条4項，GATT11条1項及びTRIMS 2条に反する[15]と考え，協議が不調に終わった後，パネルの設置を要請した.

GATT11条1項には以下のように規定されていた.

---

(12)　Report of the Panel, India-Measures Affecting the Automotive Sector, WT/DS146/R; WT/DS175/R, 21 December 2001.

(13)　Id. at 3, para.2.4.

(14)　現地化要件―各乗用車製造業者は組立キットの最初の輸入の日から3年以内に最低50%，及び5年以内に70%の現地化の達成しなければならない．Ibid., para.2.5.

(15)　Id. at 101, para.7.3.

「締約国は，他の締約国の領域の産品の**輸入について**，又は他の締約国の領域に仕向られる産品の輸出若しくは輸出のための販売について，割当によると，輸入又は輸出の許可によると，その他の措置によるとを問わず，関税その他の課徴金以外のいかなる禁止又は制限も新設し，又は維持してはならない.」(16)

(GATT Article XI 1. No prohibitions or restrictions other than duties; taxes or other charges, whether made effective through quotas; import or export licences or other measures; shall be instituted or maintained by any contracting party *on the importation* of any product of the territory of any other contracting party or on the exportation or sale for export of any product destined for the territory of any other contracting party.)

インドは，「GATT11条が規律するのは国境措置（border measures）であり，了解覚書における貿易収支均衡要件についての規定は，物品がインドの税関に入ること，つまり輸入というプロセスに影響を与えないので，GATT11条1項の『輸入に対する制限』（restrictions on importation）に当たらない.」と主張した(17).

パネルは，インドの主張を分析する前提として，GATT11条1項が規律するのはインドが主張したように国境措置（border measures）だけであるかどうかを検討した．この検討は，主に“on”の辞書の意味に基づいてなされたものである．パネルは，「Webster's New Encyclopedic Dictionary（1994年版）によると，“on”には“with respect to”，“in connection; association or activity with or with regard to”等いくつかの意味が含まれている.」と指摘した．そして，それに基づいて文脈と目的を分析した上で，

---

(16)　条約邦訳は，小寺彰＝中川淳司編・前掲第Ⅰ章注(15) 153, 154頁参照.

(17)　Report of the Panel, supra note 100, at 148 & 155, para.7.218 & para.7.255.

GATT11条1項に定められた「輸入に対する制限」(restrictions on importation)は「輸入と関係する，輸入と関わる制限」(a restriction "with regard to" or "in connection with" the importation)という意味であり，輸入のプロセスと直接関わる措置に限らず，輸入に関する他の措置も含むはずである，と判断した(18).

パネルがこの事件で行った"on"の意味についての検討結果は，ドミニカのタバコの輸入と国内販売に影響を与える措置事件とEUの砂糖への輸出補助金事件にも利用された.

② ドミニカのタバコの輸入と国内販売に影響を与える措置事件(19)

2003年，ホンジュラスは，ドミニカの 輸入品全般に対する2%の経済安定経過的課徴金，輸入品全般に対する10%の外国為替手数料，タバコ包装への税印紙貼付義務付け法令，タバコ輸入者に対する税支払確保のための保証提出義務付け(20)等の7つの政策がGATT2条，3条と11条の規定に違反するとして，パネルの設置を要請した.

パネルは，ドミニカの「タバコ輸入者に対する税支払確保のための保証提出義務付け」の政策がGATT11条1項の規定に違反するかどうかという問題を検討する際，インドの自動車部門における貿易と投資に係る措置事件においてパネルが行った"on"についての分析を，利用した．パネルは，「輸入上の制限」(restriction ... on importation)は「輸入方面の，輸入に関する制限」であるが，ドミニカの「タバコ輸入者に対する税支払確保のための保証提出義務付

---

(18) Id. at 155, para.7.257.

(19) Report of the Panel, Dominican Republic – Measures Affecting the Importation and Internal Sale of Cigarettes, WT/DS302/R, 26 November 2004.

(20) なお松下満雄＝清水章雄＝中川淳司『ケースブック：WTO法』(有斐閣，2009) 142頁 (川島富士雄) 参照.

け」の政策は特にタバコの輸入に関する政策であることが証明できないため，GATT11条1項に当たらない，と判断した(21)．結局パネルは，ドミニカの政策は他のGATTの条項に違反することはあるが，GATT11条1項には違反しないと判断した．

③ EUの砂糖への輸出補助金事件(22)

EUの砂糖への輸出補助金事件においても，パネルはインドの自動車部門における貿易と投資に係る措置事件で行った“on”の意味の分析を，利用した．ただ，その目的は前の2つの事件とは異なり，EUの砂糖への輸出補助金が農業協定9.1条に違反するかを判断することにあった．

農業協定9.1条（輸出補助金に関する約束）の(c)項は以下のように規定する(23)．

「(c)：政府の措置によって農業品の**輸出について**行われる支払（当該農産品又はその原料である農産品に対する課徴金による収入から行われる支払を含むものとし，公的勘定による負担があるかないかを問わない．）」

原文では“The following export subsidies are subject to reduction commitments under this Agreement:
— (c) payments *on the export* of an agricultural product that are financed by virtue of governmental action; whether or not a charge on the public account is involved; including payments that are financed from the proceeds of a levy imposed on the agricultural product concerned or on an agricultural product from which the exported product is derived; ”とある．

2003年，オーストラリア，ブラジルとタイは，ECが砂糖市場の

---

(21) Report of the Panel, supra note 107, at 172f., para.7.258 & para.7.259.

(22) Report of the Panel, European Communities - Export Subsidies On Sugar Complaint By Australia, WT/DS265/R, 15 October 2004.

(23) 条約邦訳は，小寺 = 中川編・前掲第Ⅰ章注(15) 13頁参照．

共通組織（Common Organization，CMO）に基づいて域内の砂糖産業に交付する輸出補助金が農業協定，補助金相殺措置協定に違反すると主張し，協議が不調となった結果，3国はパネルの設置を要請した．

ECでは，1968年砂糖市場の共通組織が設立された．現行制度は，2001年6月19日の理事会規則No.1260/2001による．この制度においては，3種類の砂糖，A糖，B糖，C糖が設けられた．A糖とB糖は生産割当量の制限があるが，国内で販売する際に介入価格の保障があり，輸出するときには輸出払戻金も給付される．また，この制度においては，A糖とB糖の精糖業者がA糖とB糖の原材料の生産業者，ビートの生産業者から原材料を購入するときの最低価格も設けられている．国内販売の介入価格と原材料購入の最低価格は，相当高いレベルで定められている．A糖，B糖の生産割当を超えて生産される砂糖がC糖である．C糖は生産割当，輸出払戻金の対象とならないほか，C糖の生産業者がC糖の原材料，Cビートを購入するときの最低価格なども定められていなかった．また，C糖は全部輸出しなければならない．輸出しないC糖には，罰金が課される(24)．輸出しなければならないという意味で国際競争に直面しているC糖の価格は，A糖とB糖に比べて比較的低い．Cビートの生産業者は生産コストを下回る価格でC糖の生産業者にCビートを売り渡す(25)ことさえある．ところがここで注意すべきなのは，A，Bビートの生産業者は同時にCビートの生産業者でもあることである．

申立国は，ECの砂糖制度が，A糖，B糖及びA，Bビートに対する介入価格や最低価格などを設けることによって，A糖，B糖及びA，Bビートの高い価格を維持するとともに，C糖とCビート

---

(24)　Report of the Panel, supra note 110, at 7f., para.3.4.

(25)　Id. at 168f., para.7.247.

の価格を低く抑えることを可能にすると認定して，ECの砂糖制度は実際には交差補助金となり，農業協定9.1(c)に定められる「政府による輸出に対する支払行為」(a payment on the export financed by virtue of governmental action) に当たる，と指摘した．その上で，以上の補助金はECの譲許表に含まれていないから，ECの砂糖制度が農業協定9.1条(c)に違反すると主張した(26)．

パネルは，ECの砂糖制度が農業協定9.1(c)に定められる「政府による輸出に対する支払行為」であるかどうかを判断するにあたって，以下の3つの点に分けて分析を行うことにした．

「1　支払 (payment) になるかどうか
2　輸出に関するかどうか (on the export)
3　政府出資の行動であるかどうか (financed by virtue of governmental action)」

パネルは，2番目の「輸出に関するかどうか」(on the export) という点を分析する際に，インドの自動車部門における貿易と投資に係る措置事件で行った "on" についての分析を利用して，"on the export" の意味は「輸出に付随的な」(contingent) という狭い意味ではなく，「輸出に関する」(in connection with exports) という広い意味であると認定した(27)．C糖の生産者は同時にA糖B糖の生産者であり，Cビートの生産業者は同時にA，Bビートの生産業者であるから，政府によるA糖B糖またはA，Bビートへの補助と，C糖の生産及び輸出との関係を，否定することはできないのである．パネルは「支払 (payment) になるかどうか」，「政府出資の行動であるかどうか (financed by virtue of governmental action)」という2つの点も分析した上で，ECの砂糖制度は実際には交差補助金となり，農業協定9.1(c)に含まれる「政府による輸出に対する支払行

(26)　Id. at 170, para.7.252.
(27)　Id. at 174, para.7.274.

為」である，と認定した(28).

以上②と③の2つの事件で，パネルは，インドの自動車部門における貿易と投資に係る措置事件で行った“on”についての分析を利用したが，中国の自動車部品の輸入に関連する措置事件では，パネルは別の方法で，条約における“on”の意味を解釈した.

④ 中国の自動車部品の輸入に関連する措置事件(29)

2006年に，EU，米国，カナダは，中国の税関総署，国家発展・改革委員会などの国家部門によって制定，実施された自動車部品輸入に関する一連の政策及び管理弁法が，GATT3条2項の「内国税」に係る規定などに反する，と主張した．彼らの要請に基づいてパネルが設置された．中国の政策において，自動車部品の輸入手続きは下のように定められている.

『自動車部品の輸入者は，物品を輸入する際に，まず税関に届出をして納税金額総担保を預託する．その時は，輸入者は関税を納付する必要はない．完成車を組み立てた後，完成車に使われた輸入部品が完成車の特徴を備えるかどうかによって，完成車税率又は部品の税率を適用し，関税と輸入増値税を徴収する(30).』

---

(28) Id. at 189, para.7.340.

(29) Reports of the Panel, China—Measures affecting Imports of Automobile Parts WT/DS339/R; WT/DS340R; WT/DS342/R, 18 July 2008.

(30) 「完成車の特徴を構成する自動車部品輸入管理弁法」(第125号令)，2005年2月28日，21条，22条.

自動車部品が，完成車として認定される場合の基準は，以下の通りである.

「1 CKDまたはSKD118部品を輸入し，自動車をアセンブリ生産する場合.

2.1 ボディー（運転席を含む），エンジンの2大モジュール（複数の部品を組み込んだユニット）を輸入し，組立生産する場合.

2.2 ボディー（運転席を含む），及びエンジンの2大モジュールの一つ，そして，その他の3つ以上の主要モジュールの部品を輸入し，自動車を組立生産する場合.

この事件における1つの争点は，中国の措置がGATT2条に規定された「通常の関税」措置であるか，それとも3条に規定された「内国税」措置であるかということである．

中国は，中国の措置がGATT2条に規定された「通常の関税」措置であると主張した．中国は，「自動車部品輸入についての規定は，不法分子が完成車と部品との税差を利用して税関の監督管理から逃れ，関税を逃れることを防止するためのものであり，GATT2条に違反しない」，「中国の措置がパネルにGATT2条1項の規定に違反すると認定されるとしても，GATT20条により正当化されるはずである」と主張した．中国がそのように主張する主な理由は，中国の措置が輸入に関する措置であることである．中国は，「GATT2条1項の「通常の関税」は“on their importation”と文脈を構成するから，輸入を条件とする，或いは輸入に関する税金徴収措置であれば「通常の関税」措置である．税金がいつどこで課されるかは関係ない.」と主張した．

GATT2条1項(b)は下のように定めている．

2.3 ボディー（運転席を含む），及びエンジンの2大モジュール以外の，その他5つ以上の主要モジュールの部品を輸入し，自動車を組立生産する場合．

3 輸入部品の価格総額が同モデル完成車価格の60%以上を占める場合．

4.1 自動車全体のバラ部品を組み立てたものである場合．

4.2 キーパーツ，もしくはモジュールを分割したものを輸入し，組み立てたものであり，その輸入したキーパーツもしくはモジュールの部品が規定の数量基準を超過する場合.」

以上のいずれかに該当する輸入自動車部品は，完成車の特徴を備えたものと見なされ，完成車税率が適用され，関税と輸入増値税を徴収されるのである．以上につき，日本貿易振興機構（JETRO）「中国の完成車特徴認定制度」2005年4月21日

http://www.rieti.go.jp/wto-c/050428/050428-1.pdf 及び「完成車の特徴を構成する自動車部品輸入管理弁法」の日本語全文訳を参考とした．
http://www.jetro.go.jp/world/asia/cn/law/pdf/trade_019.pdf

「いずれかの締約国の譲許表の第一部に掲げる産品に該当する他の締約国の領域の産品は，その譲許表が**関係する領域への輸入に際し**，その譲許表に定める条件又は制限に従うことを条件として，その譲許表に定める関税をこえる通常の関税を免除される.」(31)（The products described in Part I of the Schedule relating to any contracting party, which are the products of territories of other contracting parties, shall, *on their importation into the territory* to which the Schedule relates, and subject to the terms, conditions or qualifications set forth in that Schedule, be exempt from ordinary customs duties in excess of those set forth and provided therein.）

WTOの協定の中には，「通常の関税」の定義はない．パネルも，「通常の関税」の文脈を構成する“on their importation”の“on”から，「通常の関税」の意味を判断することにしたのである．ところが本件においてパネルは，前の3件とは異なって，条約の異なる言語の正文における対応する用語の意味の比較を通じて“on”の意味を確定することにした．パネルは，まずThe Shorter Oxford English Dictionary（2002版）とThe Webster's New Encyclopedic Dictionary（2003年版）を参照し，“on”は主に「行動発生の厳密な時間を表すもの」と「行動の条件との関係を表すもの」の2つの意味があると指摘した(32)．前者の意味は提訴国側の理解であり，

(31) 条約邦訳は，小寺＝中川編・前掲第Ⅰ章注(15) 148頁参照.

(32) The Shorter Oxford English Dictionary（2002版），には“on / preposition. ... II Of time, or action implying time. 6 During, or at some time during (a specified day or part of a day); contemporaneously with (an occasion). Also (now chiefly US & Austral.) in or at (any period of time); dial. & US used redundantly with tomorrow, yesterday. b Within the space of; in (a length of time). c Exactly at or just coming up to (a specified time), just before or after in time. 7 On the occasion of (an action); immediately after (and because of or in reaction to), as a result

後者の意味は中国側の理解である．パネルは，ウィーン条約法条約33条の規則に基づき，英語版と等しく権威を有するGATT協定のフランス語版とスペイン語版の正文における“on”と対応する用語の意味によって，“on”を解釈することにした．フランス語版の正文において“on”と対応するのは“À”であり(33)，スペイン語版の正文において“on”と対応するのは“al”である(34)．パネルは，フランス語の辞書Le Grand Robert de la langue française（1985年版）(35)

---

of.”とあり，また，

The Webster's New Encyclopedic Dictionary（2003年版）には，“on / prep … 4: with respect to <agreed on a price> 5a: in connection, association, or activity with or with regard to <on a committee> <on a tour> b in a state or process of <on fire> <on the increase> 6: during or at a specified time <every hour on the hour> <cash on delivery>”とある．なお，Reports of the Panel, supra note 117, at 189, para.7.156 & para.7.157を見よ．

(33) GATT2.1(b): “Les produits repris dans la première partie de la liste d'une partie contractante et qui sont les produits du territoire d'autres parties contractantes ne seront pas soumis, à leur importation sur le territoire auquel se rapporte cette liste et compte tenu des conditions ou clauses spéciales qui y sont stipulées, à des droits de douane proprement dits plus élevés que ceux de cette liste.”

Reports of the Panel, supra note 117, at 190, para.7.160参照．

(34) GATT2.1(b): “Los productos enumerados en la primera parte de la lista relativa a una de las partes contratantes, que son productos de los territorios de otras partes contratantes, no estarán sujetos -al ser importados en el territorio a que se refiera esta lista y teniendo en cuenta las condiciones o cláusulas especiales establecidas en ella- a derechos de aduana propiamente dichos que excedan de los fijados en la lista.” (emphasis added). Reports of the Panel, supra note 117, at 190, para.7.162参照．

(35) “À

TEMPS.

- 1. Indiquant la situation ponctuelle dans le temps, le moment.

とスペイン語の辞書 Esbozo de una Nueva Gramática de la Lengua Española, Gramática Descriptiva de la Lengua Española, el Diccionario de uso del Español（1987 年版）を調べて，“À” と “al” 双方が厳密な時間の意味を有する，と認定した．パネルはこれに基づいて，英語版 GATT 2 条 1 項における “on” の意味も「行動発生の厳密な時間を表す」ことである，と主張した．そして，条項の文脈や趣旨及び目的を分析した上で，輸入された物品の通常の関税は輸入された時に決められるべきであり，中国の自動車部品輸入に関する措置によって，徴収する税金は完成車を組み立てた後決められるから，その税は GATT2 条に規定された「通常の関税」ではない，と判断した．

中国は，インドの自動車部門における貿易と投資に係る措置事件でのパネルの “on” についての分析を利用してパネルの判断に反論したが，申立国は，インドの事件においてパネルが GATT11 条 1 項の通常の意味，文脈，趣旨及び目的を参照して下した結論を自動的に GATT2 条 1 項の解釈に適用することはできない，と主張した．パネルは申立国の意見に同意した(36)．

(3) 恣意的利用の恐れ

以上のように，中国の自動車部品の輸入に関連する措置事件で，パネルは異なる言語の正文での「対応する」用語の意味を対比することによって，英語版の条約正文における用語の意味を判断した．

---

[a] Avec un verbe ou un nom d’action. Arriver, venir, rentrer... à l’aube, au soir, à la nuit. Ils sont venus à l’époque, au moment, à l’instant où..., au moment dit, prévu, à l'heure dite.

[b] Mod. Avec un nom d'action (ci-dessus) ou un repère temporel. à l'annonce de... à ces mots, à ce signal, telle chose se passa.”

Le Grand Robert de la langue française (deuxième édition, 1985, page 3). Reports of the Panel, supra note 117, at 190, para.7.161 参照.

(36) Reports of the Panel, supra note 117, at 195, para.7.176.

この方法が適当であるかどうかは後で議論するが，ここでまず注意すべきなのは，パネルが同じ用語“on”を解釈するにあたって，従前と異なる意味の選択方法を採用した理由を，はっきり示していないことである．

ここから，次のような疑問が生じる．パネルが前の3つの事件と同じように，辞書の意味に基づいて用語の通常の意味を判断した上で，文脈および趣旨・目的を考慮して条約を解釈していたら，前の3つの事件と同じ結論を下したのか．辞書を参照する方法ではそうならざるを得ないから，異なる結論に達するために異なる解釈方法を選んだのか．もしそうであれば，パネルは前もって決めた判断に達するために解釈方法を選んだ，つまり，結論ありきの解釈方法を採ったと言えるのではないか．

アメリカ連邦最高裁判所では，1830年から，憲法，法律や紛争となる法律文書，契約の条項における用語を解釈するために，辞書を利用し始めた(37)．また興味深いことに，イギリスでもアメリカでも，裁判所が判決を下すとき，極めて簡単な用語の意味を確認するために辞書を利用することが多くなっている(38)．2009年と2010年の最高裁判所の判決では，“assist”，“arrange”，“care”，“relief”，“oppose”，“now”，“also”，“any”，“if”といった用語も，辞書の意味を利用して解釈されている．また，「数から見ると，裁判において解釈が必要となる用語は，実は難語より皆が普段から慣れ親しんでいる用語の方が多い．だからそれはおかしいことではない．」ということも指摘された(39)．

だが，ここで疑問なのは，なぜ簡単な語についても辞書の意味を

(37) Jeffrey L. Kirchmeier / Samuel Thumma, supra note 82, at 79.

(38) Id. at 101f.
Roderick Munday, The Bridge That Choked a Watercourse or Repetitive Dictionary Disorder, STATUTE L.REV.29(1)(2008), at 35.

(39) Jeffrey L. Kirchmeier / Samuel Thumma, supra note 82, at 101f.

利用する必要があるのかということである．既に本稿の第Ⅱ章の最後で論じたように，辞書を利用して「文脈により且つその趣旨及び目的に照らして与えられえる用語の通常の意味に従い……解釈する」ことの裏には，一種の恣意性が隠されていた．つまり，「誠実に解釈する」とは言えない営みが，ここに隠されているかもしれないのである．また，皆が普段から慣れている用語，特に助動詞，冠詞，前置詞などの辞書の意味は，あまりにも広すぎるため，恣意的な選択の恐れが一層高い，と考えられる．

3　ウィーン条約法条約33条3項と辞書の利用

パネルの報告書と上級委員会の報告書を見ると，条約を解釈するときにウィーン条約法条約33条3項によって辞書を利用することが多くなっている．ここで問題となるのは，ウィーン条約法条約33条3項が条約解釈方法となることの正当性である．

(1)　いくつかの実例

既に本章の前に紹介した中国の自動車部品の輸入に関連する措置事件では，更に若干の議論があった．パネルは，中国の政策がGATT2条1項で規律する「通常の関税」措置であるかどうかを判断するにあたって，“on”の意味を確定するために，条約のスペイン語版とフランス語版の正文で“on”と対応する用語の辞書における意味を利用することにしたのである．また，米国のカナダからの軟材に対する相殺関税決定事件と米国の国境を越えた賭博サービス規制措置事件においても，パネルと上級委員会が条約を解釈するときに同じような方法を採用していた．

米国のカナダからの軟材に対する相殺関税決定事件においては，パネルは辞書における「物品」（goods）の意味に基づいて，「物品の概念は広範なので，立木（standing timber）も含むはずである」

と主張した[40]が，これに対してカナダが上訴した．上級委員会は，この問題を分析するにあたって，フランス語版，スペイン語版の補助金及び相殺措置に関する協定を対比した．フランス語版の補助金及び相殺協定において“goods”と対応するのは“biens”であり，スペイン語版の協定においては“bienes”である．上級委員会は，フランス語の辞書 le Nouveau Petit Robert（2003）とスペイン語の辞書 el Diccionario de la Lengua Española（2001）とを調べて，辞書によるとこの２つの用語は，いずれも広く「財産」の意味であり，「動産」と「不動産」両方の意味を有していること，つまり，移動できない財産も含むことを確認した．それによって上級委員会は，パネルの「物品」（goods）についての広い解釈はスペイン語の正文とフランス語の正文における対応する用語の意味と一致しているとして，パネルの判断を支持した[41]．

米国の国境を越えた賭博サービス規制措置事件で，米国の自由化約束表において除外される「スポーティング」（sporting）には賭博が含まれるかを判断する際，パネルは，まず The Shorter Oxford English Dictionary (1993), Merriam-Webster Dictionary Online, The Oxford English Dictionary (1938), The Penguin Pocket English Dictionary (1988), The New Oxford Thesaurus of English 等の辞書を調べて，「スポーティング」の意味を確認した[42]．パネルは，「『スポーティング』の意味に賭博を含める辞書と賭博を含めない辞書の両方があるが，賭博の意味が含まれるとき，それには軽蔑的な意味があって，主に賭博が好きな人を表すために使われることになり，サービス活動を表現する最も適切な用語ではない」

---

(40)　Report of the Panel,supra note 61, at 78f., paras.7.23 & 7.24.

(41)　Report of the Appellate Body , United States - Final Countervailing Duty Determination with Respect to Certain Softwood Lumber from Canada, WT/DS257/AB/R, 19 January 2004, at 21f., para.59.

(42)　Report of the Panel, supra note 67, at 151ff., paras.6.54-6.58.

と判断した(43)．その上でパネルは，フランス語とスペイン語の辞書を調べて，フランス語版とスペイン語版の翻訳の中で「スポーティング」と対応する“sportifs”と“deportivos”の意味には賭博が含まれない，ということを確認した(44)．以上の検討を通じて，パネルは，「スポーティング」の通常の意味には賭博は入らないと結論づけた．

(2)　英，仏，西語の比較検討による解釈方法の根拠

WTOの公式言語は英語，フランス語，スペイン語の3つである(45)．WTOの協定，例えば「世界貿易機関を設立するマラケシュ協定」，「GATT協定」にも，「等しく正文である英語，フランス語及びスペイン語により……作成した」等の定めが設けられている(46)．そして，「2以上の言語により確定された条約の解釈」に関するウィーン条約法条約33条においては，下のように定められている(47)．

「1　条約について二以上の言語により確定がされた場合には，

---

(43)　Id. at 153, para.6.59.

(44)　Id. at 153, para.6.60.

(45)　WTO公式ホームページ参照．アクセス：2012年1月20日．
http://wto.org/english/thewto_e/vacan_e/recruit_e.htm

(46)　条約邦訳は，小寺＝中川編・前掲第Ⅰ章注(15)6，7頁参照．なお，それぞれの原文は，以下の通り．

Marrakesh Agreement Establishing the World Trade Organization Article XVI(6)：

“DONE at Marrakesh this fifteenth day of April one thousand nine hundred and ninety-four, in a single copy, in the English, French and Spanish languages, each text being authentic.”

General Agreement on Tariffs and Trade 1994 2 (c)(i)

“The text of GATT 1994 shall be authentic in English, French and Spanish.”

(47)　奥脇直也編・前掲第Ⅰ章注(13)122頁．

それぞれの言語による条約文がひとしく権威を有する．ただし，相違があるときは特定の言語による条約文によることを条約が定めている場合又はこのことについて当事国が合意する場合は，この限りでない．

2　条約文の確定に係る言語以外の言語による条約文は，条約に定めがある場合又は当事国が合意する場合にのみ，正文とみなされる．

3　条約の用語は，各正文において同一の意味を有すると推定される．

4　1の規定に従い特定の言語による条約文による場合を除くほか，各正文の比較により，第31条及び前条の規定を適用しても解消されない意味の相違があることが明らかとなった場合には，条約の趣旨及び目的を考慮した上，すべての正文について最大の調和が図られる意味を採用する．」

パネルと上級委員会は，しばしばウィーン条約法条約33条，特に33条3項を利用して，英語，フランス語，スペイン語の比較検討によってある文言を解釈した．また，この比較検討はほとんどが辞書の意味に基づいてなされたものである．メキシコのBradly J.Condon教授が，この比較検討による解釈方法について，興味深い統計を示している[48]．

まず上級委員会の報告書について見ると，2009年までに上級委員会が出した報告書の中でウィーン条約法条約33条に言及したのは7件だった．当事国がどちらも正文間の対照をしなかったにもかかわらず，上級委員会がウィーン条約法条約33条に言及せずに各正文を対照したのは，6件だった．少なくとも1つの当事国が正文

⑷⑻ Bradly J.Condon , Lost in Translatioin: A comparative Analysis of Plurilingual Interpretion in WTO Panel and Appellate Body Reports.
http://cdei.itam.mx/medios_digitales/archivos/investigacion/Condon-PanelAB.pdf

を対照したのは12件だった．また，パネル報告書について見ると，1999年から2009年までに出された106件のパネル報告書の中で，少なくとも1つの当事国或いはパネルが正文を対照したのは52件だった．

前記の(1)に挙げられた3つの事件で条約を解釈するときも，パネルや上級委員会は，根拠としてウィーン条約法条約33条3項の「条約の用語は，各正文において同一の意味を有すると推定される」との文言と「解釈は，条約のすべての文言に意味及び効果を与えなくてはならない」との実効的解釈の原則（effective interpretation）を挙げた(49)．また，パネルは，ウィーン条約法条約を起草する国際法委員会が1966年国連大会への最終草案の報告の中で述べた「各正文において条約の用語が等しく意味を有しているという仮定は，どの言語に依るかを選択する前に，テキストの共通の意味を求めるためにあらゆる努力をすることを要求する.」との意見，そして国際司法裁判所の判決も，利用した．

このようなパネルの理解によれば，ウィーン条約法条約33条3項は，すでに1つの独立の解釈方法として採用されたことになる．しかし，パネルや上級委員会のこのような解釈方法は，これで本当に正当化されるのか．

ここでカギとなるのは，ウィーン条約法条約33条3項をいかに理解すべきか，ということである．国際法委員会がウィーン条約法条約を起草するときの年報によると，今のウィーン条約法条約31条と32条の解釈規則の内容がおおよそ確定された後で，ある専門家が2つ以上の言語の正文の比較対照を，解釈規則として31条に入れることを提案した(50)．しかし，特別報告者たるHumphrey

---

(49)　Report of the Panel, supra note 67, at 149ff., paras. 6.45-6.49; Report of the Appellate Body, supra note 129, at 21f., para.59; Report of the Panel, supra note 117, at 191f., para. 7.165.

(50)　Yearbook of the International Law Commission (1966), Vol. I, at 209,

WALDOCK 教授は反対の意見を表した．WALDOCK 教授の挙げた主な理由は3つである．1つ目は，「それぞれの言語には，それぞれの特徴がある．異なる言語では，いつも同じ表現と文法で同じ意味を表せるわけではない．……このやり方は，ある言語のテキストを解釈するときに別の言語の概念を移植することを助長し，意味を歪曲する可能性がある.」(51)というものである．2つ目は，「(正文間の）比較対照を法的解釈方法として……条項に入れれば，問題が生じない場合にも1つの言語の正文を締約国の意図の表れとしてとらえることができなくなり，締約国の意図を知るために全ての正文を見なければならないことになる」というものである．3つ目は，

---

para.8 ; Vol. Ⅱ , at 100, para.23.

(51) 原文で示せば，“Each language has its own genius, and it is not always possible to express the same idea in identical phraseology or syntax in different languages. It is one thing to admit interaction between two versions when each has been interpreted in accordance with its own genius and a divergence has appeared between them or an ambiguity in one of them. But it is another thing to attribute legal value to a comparison for the purpose of determining the ordinary meaning of the terms in the context of the treaty; for this may encourage attempts to transplant concepts of one language into the interpretation of a text in another language with a resultant distortion of the meaning.”

Yearbook of the International Law Commission, supra note 138, Vol. II, at100, para.23. とある．なお，「ガッツが取り扱う事項は，物品とは異なって多種多様なものが含まれており，……これらにおいては，自国語以外の言語では適切に表現されえないものもあり得ると考えられる．……英，仏，西語の文字の辞書的解釈に過度に依存することには限界もあろう.」とする．松下満雄「「米国の国境を越えた賭博サービスの及ぼす影響に係る措置」上級委員会報告」『ガット・WTO の紛争処理に関する調査　調査報告書ＸⅥ』（2005 年）136 頁をも参照せよ．

http://www.meti.go.jp/policy/trade_policy/wto/pdf/ds/panelreport/2005/matsushita.pdf

この解釈方法を採用すれば，国際条約を起草するための外国語に精通する人が少ない最近の独立国が，実際上の困難に直面することになる，という点である[52]．そのため，WALDOCK教授は，複数の言語の正文がある条約については，それぞれの言語独自の特徴によって解釈し，相違が生じる場合には相互の参照が認められるが，異なる言語の比較対照によってある文言の通常の意味を確定することを法的解釈方法として位置づけることはできない.」と主張した[53]．WALDOCK教授の意見は多くの国からの賛同を得て，結局異なる言語の正文間の比較対照は，解釈規則としてウィーン条約法条約31条には，入れられなかったのである．

国際法委員会は，1966年国連大会への最終草案の報告の中で，ウィーン条約法条約33条に関連して，条約の一体性を強調した．国際法委員会は，「たとえ2つの正文が異なるように見えても，法律上はただ1つの条約──締約国の同意を得たひとそろいの条項とその条項に関する1つの共通意思──が存在している.」[54]，「異なる

(52) "To erect comparison into one of the means of legal interpretation set out in article 69 would imply that it was no longer possible to rely on a single text as an expression of the will of the parties until a difficulty arose and that it was necessary to consult all the authentic texts for that purpose; such a procedure would have a number of drawbacks and would, in particular, involve practical difficulties for the legal advisers of the newly independent States, who did not always have staff familiar with the many languages used in drafting international treaties."

Yearbook of the International Law Commission Vol. I, supra note 138, at 211, para.35.

(53) Yearbook of the International Law Commission Vol. II, supra note 138, at100, para.23.

(54) "But it needs to be stressed that in law there is only one treaty—one set of terms accepted by the parties and one common intention with respect to those terms—even when two authentic texts appear to di-

言語の正文がある条約の解釈において最も重要なのは，条約と各条項の一体性である．この一体性は，各正文が等しく権威を有するという原則と，各正文の用語は同一の意味を有するよう意図されているという仮定によって，守られている．この仮定は，どの言語に依るかを選択する前に，テキストの共通の意味を確定するためにあらゆる努力が行われることを要求する．」(55)と述べた．このように，国際法委員会は「テキストの共通の意味を確定するためにあらゆる努力をすることを要求する」という意見を提示した．

WTO紛争において当事国やパネル，上級委員会はこの意見に基づいて異なる言語の正文間の比較対照を解釈方法として採用したのだが，しかしながらそれは，国際法委員会が意図したことではなかった．まず，国際法委員会の「ウィーン条約法条約33条1項と3項」についての，「各正文が等しく権威を有することと各正文の用語が同一の意味を有することが，条約の一体性を保証する」という意見からすると，既述の如く，ウィーン条約法条約33条3項は，実は，『条約を解釈するとき，各正文は等しく権威を有していて，各正文の用語も同一の意味を有しているから，異なる言語の正文間での比較対照をする必要はない』という意味だったのである．そして，もしそれぞれの言語独自の特徴によって条約を解釈した結果相違が生じる場合，「ただ1つの条約──締約国の同意を得たひとそろいの条項とその条項に関する1つの共通意思──が存在している」のだから，「テキストの共通の意味を確定するためあらゆる努力を

---

verge." Id. at 225, para.(6).

(55) "The unity of the treaty and of each of its terms is of fundamental importance in the interpretation of plurilingual treaties and it is safeguarded by combining with the principle of the equal authority of authentic texts the presumption that the terms are intended to have the same meaning in each text. This presumption requires that every effort should be made to find a common meaning for the texts before preferring one to another." Ibid., para.(7).

することを要求する」のである．また，どういうふうにテキストの共通の意味を確定するかについては，国際法委員会はウィーン条約31条と32条の解釈方法に従わなければならないと主張した(56)．国際法委員会の意見によれば，「複数の正文の存在を認めることが，条約解釈に正文の対比という新たな要素を持ち込むことになるのは，明白である．しかしそれは異なる解釈システムを伴うものではない(57)」．条約の解釈方法として認められるのは，ウィーン条約法条約31条と32条しかないのである．ウィーン条約法条約33条3項は，条約の解釈方法というより，むしろ異なる言語の正文を有する条約解釈の，前提なのである．

かくて，辞書における英語，フランス語，スペイン語の「対応」する用語の比較検討によってある文言を解釈する根拠はなくなった．のみならず，異なる条約解釈の「国際法上の慣習的規則」を組み合わせることによって，新しい条約解釈方法を作り出すことができるかどうかについても，疑問があるということになる．

以上のさしあたりの分析によって，英語，フランス語，スペイン語の対応する用語の辞書の意味における共通点を利用して用語の通常の意味を確定し，条約を解釈する方法は，実は適当ではない，との帰結が，導かれ得るであろう．

---

(56) "Plurilingual in expression, the treaty remains a single treaty with a single set of terms the interpretation of which is governed by the rules set out in articles 27 and 28." Ibid., para.(7).

(57) "The existence of more than one authentic text clearly introduces a new element—comparison of the texts into the interpretation of the treaty. But it does not involve a different system of interpretation." Ibid., para.(7).

第Ⅳ章　辞書の利用についての意見とルール

1　辞書の利用についての上級委員会の意見

(1)　上級委員会報告書における辞書の利用

それでは，WTOの紛争処理手続きにおいて法的な問題及び法的解釈に関する上訴を審理する上級委員会は，この辞書についての様々な議論に対して，いかなる意見を有しているのか．以下では，まずいくつかの表と図を通じて，上級委員会報告書における辞書の利用の全体的状況を見て，それから上級委員会の意見を分析する．

表8と**図2**に示したのは，1996年から2010年までの各年次に採択された上級委員会報告書数，辞書を利用する報告書数，利用された辞書の種類数と報告書に利用された辞書の種類の平均値である．**表8**によると，2006年と2010年に，採択された上級委員会の報告書全てで辞書が利用されている．1996年，1999年，2003年，2004年と2009年に採択された上級委員会の報告書の中で辞書を利用しなかったのは，それぞれたった1件である．

このように，上級委員会報告書の中で辞書を利用することは一般的であるが，利用された辞書の種類はパネル報告書に比べて差が大きい．パネル報告書の中には4冊，5冊の辞書を利用した報告書も多いのに対して，各上級委員会報告書で利用された辞書はわずか1冊か2冊である．

図3は，各年次にパネル報告書と上級委員会報告書に占める辞書を利用する報告書の割合の比較である．**図4**は，各年次にパネル報告書と上級委員会報告書に利用された辞書の種類の平均値の比較で

ある．この2つの図を通じて，1996年から2010までのパネルと上級委員会報告書における辞書の利用の展開のプロセスを対照して見ることができる．**図3**を見ると，辞書を利用する上級委員会報告書の比率が終始60％の前後を変動しているのに対して，辞書を利用するパネル報告書数は1997年以後急速に増加していて，2001年，2003年，2004年，2005年，2006年，2009年の全てのパネル報告書が辞書を利用している．比率が下がることもあったが，少なくとも80％の比率は保っていた．**図4**を見ると，上級委員会が利用した辞書の種類数の平均値は低い数値で安定しているのに対し，パネルが利用した辞書の種類数の平均値は2007年を除いて上昇傾向にあり，著しい対照をなしている．

表8　各年次に採択された上級委員会報告書数，辞書を利用した報告書数，利用された辞書の種類数と報告書に利用された辞書種類の平均値(1)

年次	採択された上級委員会報告書数	辞書を利用する報告書数	利用された辞書の種類数	報告書に利用された辞書種類の平均値（小数点以下1桁まで）
1996	2	1	1	1
1997	5	2	5	2.5
1998	8	5	6	1.2
1999	8	7	16	2.3
2000	8	4	9	2.3
2001	9	7	14	2
2002	9	5	12	2.4

(1)　年次は上級委員会報告書が採択された時期を示す．合併の場合，1件として計算する．各報告書に利用された辞書種類の数を合算するが，書名と版数がはっきり示されていない辞書は不算入とする．

2003	3	2	3	1.5
2004	7	6	11	1.8
2005	8	5	9	1.8
2006	3	3	3	1
2007	3	1	2	2
2008	6	4	11	2.8
2009	2	1	1	1
2010	2	2	2	1

図 2　各年次に採択された上級委員会の報告書数，辞書を利用する報告書数と報告書に利用された辞書の種類の平均値

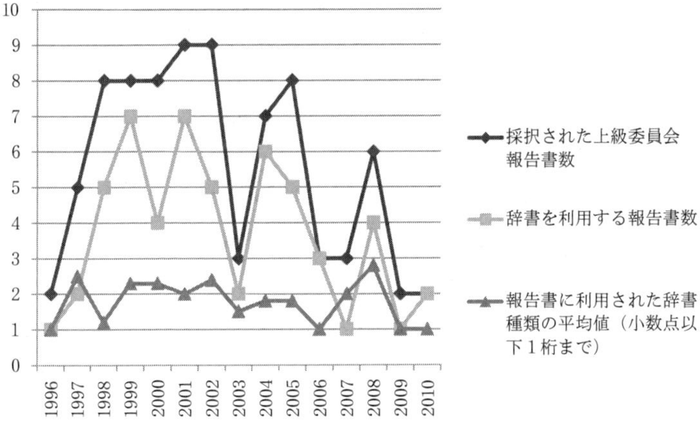

図３　各年次にパネル報告書と上級委員会報告書に占める辞書を利用した報告書の割合の比較

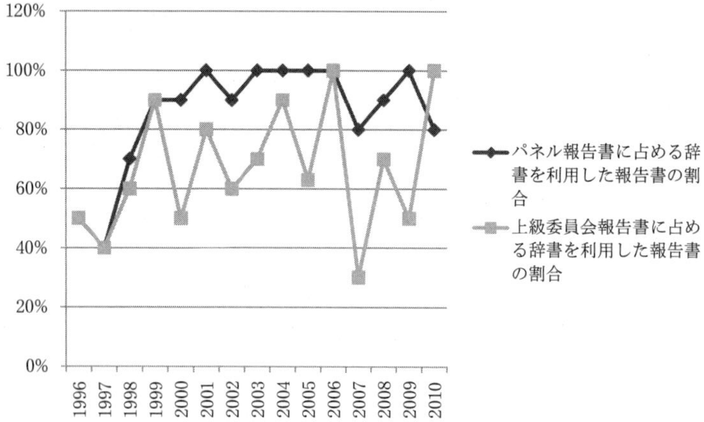

図４　各年次にパネル報告書と上級委員会報告書に利用された辞書の種類の平均値の比較

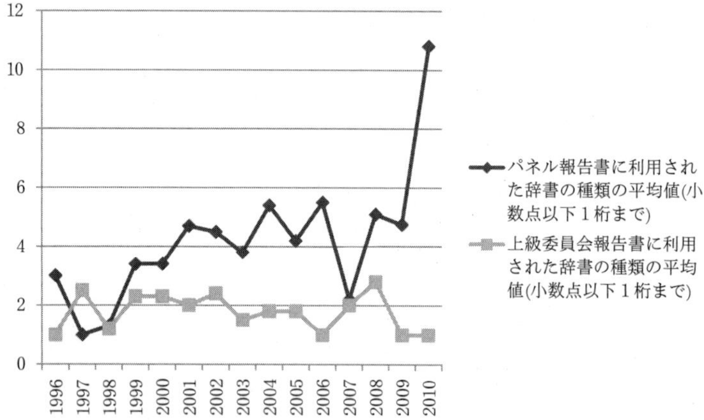

表 9 では，各年次に採択された上級委員会報告書の中で辞書を利用した報告書数，辞書の意味を利用した用語数と報告書で辞書を利用した用語数の平均値を示す．上級委員会は上訴書に提起された問題だけについて分析すればよいので，報告書において辞書の意味を利用した用語数がパネル報告書のそれに比べて少ないこと自体はおかしくない．だがここで注意すべきなのは，**図 5** と**図 4** が似ていることである．**図 5** では，**図 4** と同じように，上級委員会報告書中の辞書を利用した用語数の平均値を表す線は，比較的安定的低いレベルを保っているのに対して，パネル報告書中の辞書を利用した用語数の平均値を表す線は，2007 年の急落を除いて常に上昇を続け，次第に上級委員会の線と離れるようになっている．

表 9　各年次に採択された上級委員会報告書の中で辞書を利用した報告書数，辞書の意味を利用した用語数と報告書に辞書の意味を利用した用語数の平均値(2)

年次	辞書を利用した報告書数	辞書の意味を利用した用語数	報告書に辞書の意味を利用した用語数の平均値（小数点以下 1 桁まで）
1996	1	2	2
1997	2	3	1.5
1998	5	10	2
1999	7	21	3
2000	4	10	2.5
2001	7	22	3.1
2002	5	20	4
2003	2	4	2
2004	6	20	3.3

(2)　年次はパネル報告書が採択された時期を基準とする．合併の場合，1 件として計算する．各報告書に利用された用語の数を合算する．

2005	5	29	5.8
2006	3	5	1.7
2007	1	2	2
2008	4	19	4.8
2009	1	2	2
2010	2	12	6

図 5　各年次にパネル報告書と上級委員会報告書において辞書の意味を利用した用語数の平均値の比較

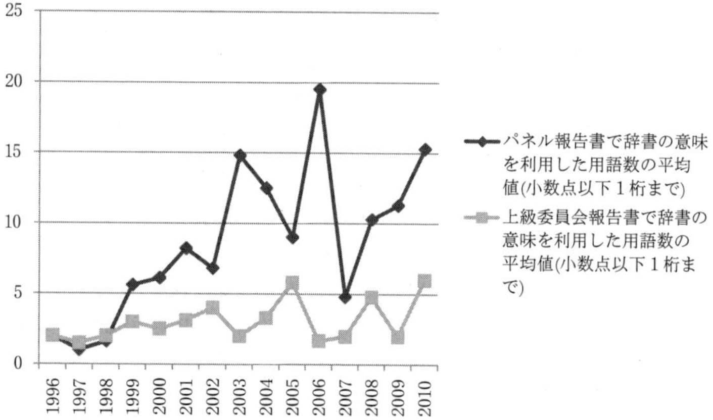

表 10 は各年次に採択された上級委員会報告書の中で辞書の意味を利用した用語を示す．パネル報告書と同じように，皆が慣れている簡単な言葉“should”，“all”，“like”，“necessary”，“any”，“might”，“as”，“to”，“base”，“laws”等も多数ある．

表10 各年次に採択された上級委員会報告書の中で辞書の意味を利用した用語(3)

年次	辞書の意味を利用した用語
1996	in conjunction with; made effective
1997	burden of proof; locus standi; standing
1998	**based on;** conceder; conform to; global annual tariff quota; likelihood; matter; potential; probability; science; scientific
1999	anticipated; application; arise; basic rationale; benefit; competitive; confer; consumer; contingent; government; payment; proceeding; proceedings; shall not prevent; **should;** substitutable; **sufficient;** thereupon; tie; to grant
2000	**available;** circumvent; commitments; de novo review; marketing; **provide;** subject matter; unforeseeable; unforeseen
2001	**all;** attribute; average; bearing; **by; cause;** comparable; competitive; cooperate; establishment; focus; investigation; **like; necessary;** objective; positive evidence; primarily; proper; realized; to weight; weighted average
2002	**against; as is;** available; based on; **basis;** convert; derogate; discrete; inappropriate; ineffective; levy; **or; ordinary;** owner; propiamente dicho; proprement dit; sardines; similar; substantiate; telle quelle
2003	conclusion; **might;** reason; result
2004	accordance; adequate; ample; as regards; consider; determine; discriminate; enterprise; generalized; goods; **in relation to;** non-discriminatory preference; notwithstanding; participation; positive; prevailing; provides; rapport; remuneration; respect
2005	**any; base;** brine; compelling; **decide;** defined and fixed base period; determine; **direct;** dried; effect; entertainment; entrust; form; grant; in brine; market; numerical; probative; quota; recreational; **related to;** salted; smoked; specific; sporting; support to a specific commodity; to dry; to smoke

(3) 用語が重複した場合，1つとして取り入れる．

2006	administer; investigation; **laws; regulations; should**
2007	**method;** provided for
2008	**authorized;** certain; critical mass; deliberations; ejusdem generis; equivalent; latency period; **likely;** proceedings; qua; reasonable; removed; suspected
2009	**as;** presented
2010	commodity; delay; distribution; distribution channel; recording; regulate; **right; to;** trade; undue; videos; without prejudice to

以上の図表によって，全体として見ると，上級委員会報告書においては辞書が頻繁に利用される一方で，ある程度のコントロールも加えられていることが分かる．その結果，上級委員会報告書における辞書の利用は比較的安定している．これに対して，パネルの報告書における辞書の利用は，上級委員会報告書における辞書の利用に比べて遅く始まったものの，急速に進展していて，すでに制御できない状態になっている．

⑵　辞書の利用についての上級委員会の意見

次に，以上を踏まえつつ，上級委員会報告書における辞書の利用について，上級委員会が具体的にどのような意見を持っているかを検討する．

1)　辞書の利用――サイレントな始まり

1996 年，上級委員会は米国－ガソリン基準事件で “made effective”，“in conjunction with” を解釈するために The New Shorter Oxford English Dictionary on Historical Principles (1993) を利用した．これにより，上級委員会は初めて辞書の利用を WTO 紛争処理手続きに導入した．ところが，上級委員会が報告書の中で

“made effective”, “in conjunction with” の通常の意味を分析するにあたっては，直接辞書の意味を利用して，利用された辞書の名前と版を注で示したのみだった．なぜ通常の意味を確定するために，上記の特定の辞書の意味を利用したのかについては，何の説明もなかったのである．さらに，96 年から 98 年までの 3 年間で辞書を利用した上級委員会の報告書は 8 件であったが，個別の辞書の利用について何の説明，指示もなく，上級委員会はずっと沈黙したままだった．

2) 「辞書の意味は多くの解釈問題を未解決のままにしておく」

1999 年に採択されたカナダ民間航空機輸出に係る措置事件の上級委員会報告書の中で，上級委員会は初めて「辞書の意味は多くの解釈問題を未解決のままにしておく」と述べた(4)．そして，2000 年に採択された米国の外国小売業者への課税制度事件の上級委員会報告書と，2001 年に採択された EU のアスベスト及びその製品に係る輸入禁止措置事件の上級委員会報告書においても，この点を繰り返した(5)．ところが，上級委員会が述べたこの言葉は，辞書の意味だけによって用語の通常の意味を判断することは「できない」という事実を示しただけであった．つまり，辞書の意味だけによって用語の通常の意味を判断「すべきではない」，という意味は，そこにはなかったのである．カナダの民間航空機輸出に係る措置事件にお

(4) “dictionary meanings leave many interpretive questions open” Report of the Appellate Body, Canada - Measures Affecting the Export of Civilian Aircraft, WT/DS70/AB/R, 2 August 1999, at 38, para.153.

(5) Report of the Appellate Body, United States - Tax Treatment for “Foreign Sales Corporations”, WT/DS108/AB/R, 24 February 2000, at 45, para.129; Report of the Appellate Body, European Communities - Measures Affecting Asbestos and Asbestos - Containing Products, WT/DS135/AB/R, 12 March 2001, at 35, para.92.

いて，上級委員会は“benefit”の辞書の意味を利用した後に自身の理解も加え，そして文脈としてSCM協定1.1(b)の中の“thereby conferred”も調べた後，条約の中の“benefit”の意味を判断した．米国の外国小売業者への課税制度事件やEUのアスベスト及びその製品に係る輸入禁止措置事件でも，それは同じである．さらに，EUのアスベスト及びその製品に係る輸入禁止措置事件においては，上級委員会が「類似」(like)を解釈するときに辞書の意味の限定性を詳しく説明した．上級委員会は，「類似」の解釈にあたっては，どのような機能が類似であるか，どの程度まで類似であるか，消費者の立場あるいは生産者の立場から類似と言えるのかを判断すべきところ，辞書の意味だけによってはそれらを判断できない(6)，と指摘した．

3）「辞書は，協定や法律文書にある用語の意味を解釈する重要な指針であって，最終的な解釈を述べたものではない」(7)

パネルが条約の解釈にあたって辞書を頻繁に利用するようになるとともに，紛争当事国が，その上訴書において，パネルが利用した辞書の定義に関わる異議を述べることも多くなった．米国の外国小売業者への課税制度事件においては，米国は，パネルが利用した“provide”の意味は“provide”の最も通常の意味ではないと指摘した(8)．また，タイのポーランド製鉄鋼に対するAD措置事件では，タイは「パネルは，AD協定3.1条の“positive evidence”を解釈するにあたり，Concise Oxford Dictionaryにおける“positive evidence”の定義を利用すべきではなく，Black's Law Dictionaryの定義を利用すべきであった．」と主張した(9)．

(6) WT/DS135/AB/R, supra note 150, at 35, para.92.
(7) Report of the Appellate Body, supra note 31, at 78f., para.248.
(8) WT/DS108/AB/R, supra note 150, at 13, para.35.
(9) Report of the Appellate Body, Thailand – Anti-Dumping Duties on

ますます多くなった辞書についての論争に対して，上級委員会は，米国2000年継続ダンピング・補助金相殺法事件報告書の中で「辞書は，協定や法律文書にある用語の意味を解釈する重要な指針であって，最終的な解釈を述べたものではない」と指摘した．

4)　米国の国境を越えた賭博サービス規制措置事件

既に論じたように，米国の国境を越えた賭博サービス規制措置事件では，パネルは米国の自由化約束表において除外される「スポーティング」(sporting) には賭博が含まれるかどうかを判断する際に多くの辞書を調べ，さらに，フランス語版とスペイン語版の翻訳の中で「スポーティング」と対応する用語 “sportifs” と “deportivos” の意味を確定するためにフランス語とスペイン語の辞書も調べた後で，「スポーティング」の通常の意味には賭博は入らない，と結論づけた．上級委員会はパネルの結論を支持したが，本件においてはパネルの条約解釈方法，特に用語の通常の意味を確定する方法は適当ではない，と指摘した．上級委員会はまず，「ウィーン条約法条約31条1項は，条約を文脈により且つその趣旨及び目的に照らして与えられる用語の通常の意味に従い誠実に解釈する，と規定する．パネルは通常の意味を確定するために辞書の意味から用語を解釈し始めるかもしれないが，辞書だけでは，必ずしも複雑な解釈問題を解決できるものではない．というのは，一般的な意味であれ，珍しい意味であれ，幅広く使われる意味であれ，専門的な意味であれ，辞書はただ用語のすべての意味を並べようとするからである．」(10)

Angles, Shapes and Sections of Iron Or Non-Alloy Steel and H-Beams from Poland, WT/DS122/AB/R, 12 March 2001, at 7, para.21.

(10) “Article 31(1) of the Vienna Convention requires a treaty to be interpreted ‘in good faith in accordance with the ordinary meaning to be given to the terms of the treaty in their context and in the light of its object and purpose.’ In order to identify the ordinary meaning, a Panel

と指摘した．そして，報告書におけるパネルの解釈方法に対して，上級委員会は「パネルが用語の通常の意味と辞書の定義を同一と見なすのはあまりに機械的な方法である……また辞書によると，ある場合には『スポーティング』に賭博が含まれることもあるから(11)，……パネルがこの段階で辞書の意味だけによって用語の意味を判断するのは早計であり，パネルは辞書によれば2つの定義があることを認めた上で更に用語の意味を確定するべきであった．」と指摘した．上級委員会はウィーン条約法条約32条を適用し，W/120及び1993年スケジューリング・ガイドライン等を準備作業に係る文書として用いて，これらと米国約束表の比較対照等を通じて米国の自由化表は賭博サービスを例外としていないと結論づけている(12)．

5）辞書の意味と「事実上の文脈」(factual context)

EUの冷凍骨なし鶏肉の関税分類事件において，EUは上訴書の中で「パネルが辞書の意味に基づいて“salted”の通常の意味を判断する際に『事実上の文脈』も一緒に考えたことは，ウィーン条約法条約の条約解釈についての規定に違反する．」と主張した(13)．上

---

may start with the dictionary definitions of the terms to be interpreted. But dictionaries, alone, are not necessarily capable of resolving complex questions of interpretation , as they typically aim to catalogue all meanings of words—be those meanings common or rare, universal or specialized.”

Report of the Appellate Body, supra note 30, at 56, para.164.

(11) “First, to the extent that the Panel's reasoning simply equates the ‘ordinary meaning’ with the meaning of words as defined in dictionaries, this is, in our view, too mechanical an approach. Secondly, the Panel failed to have due regard to the fact that its recourse to dictionaries revealed that gambling and betting can, at least in some contexts, be one of the meanings of the word ‘sporting’.” Id. at 57, para 166.

(12) 松下満雄・前掲第Ⅲ章注(51) 131頁．

(13) Report of the Appellate Body, European Communities - Customs

級委員会は「辞書は条約用語の通常の意味を分析するための有用な出発点であるが，必ずしも決定的なものではない．条約の用語の通常の意味はそれぞれの場合の特定の状況に応じて確定すべきである．重要なのは，条約の用語の通常の意味は使用する言葉で表現される当事国の意図や事件の状態に照らして見る必要があることだ．」(14)と指摘した．上級委員会はさらに，「ウィーン条約法条約31条に定められた国際法上の慣習的規則による解釈は全体的アプローチであり，機械的に硬直的な部分的作業に細分化されるべきではない…….『事実上の文脈』は，たとえ通常の意味を判断する際に考慮すべきものではなくても文脈に含まれるべきであるから，『事実上の文脈』は通常の意味を判断するために考慮すべきものであれ，文脈として考慮すべきであれ，解釈の結果は変わらない」(15)と指摘した．

6) 全体的アプローチ（holistic approach）

上級委員会は辞書の利用が過剰であることを指摘したが，実際の紛争事件においては，辞書の利用や辞書の利用についての論争は，続いていた．米国の韓国産DRAMSに対する相殺関税調査事件に

Classification of Frozen Boneless Chicken Cuts, WT/DS269/AB/R; WT/DS286/AB/R, 12 September 2005, at 7, paras.15 &16.

(14) "[D] ictionaries are a 'useful starting point' for the analysis of 'ordinary meaning' of a treaty term, but they are not necessarily dispositive. The ordinary meaning of a treaty term must be ascertained according to the particular circumstances of each case. Importantly, the ordinary meaning of a treaty term must be seen in the light of the intention of the parties 'as expressed in the words used by them against the light of the surrounding circumstances'." Id. at 69, para.175.

(15) "Interpretation pursuant to the customary rules codified in Article 31 of the Vienna Convention is ultimately a holistic exercise that should not be mechanically subdivided into rigid components." Ibid., para.176.

おいては，米国は上訴書で，パネルが一部の辞書の定義だけによって “entrust” と “directs” の意味を判断したことに対して異議を申し立てた(16)．米国のAD・相殺関税に基づくボンド指令事件においても，EUは，パネルが “suspected” の意味を解釈する際に辞書の意味を重視しすぎて，文脈等の解釈ための他の要素を無視したことを指摘した(17)．そして，中国の出版物及び音響映像製品の貿易権及び流通サービスに関する措置事件では，辞書の利用が改めて論争の焦点となった．中国は上訴書の中で，「パネルが，中国が提出した American Heritage Dictionary of the English Language（2000年版）による “recording” の意味「音声と映像を記録する媒体」（something on which sound or visual images have been recorded）を無視して，ごく一部の辞書だけによって結論を出したのは，いい加減すぎる．(18)」と指摘した．中国は，「辞書によると2つの定義があるから，パネルは辞書だけによって用語の意味を判断できないことを認めた上，文脈や条約の趣旨及び目的によって判断すべきであった．」と主張した．興味深いことに，中国の意見は，上級委員会が米国の国境を越えた賭博サービス規制措置事件で行った指摘と全く同じものだったのである．中国の意見に対して，上級委員会は，まず通常の意味を確定するための解釈方法について以下のように解説した．「パネルは辞書の意味から用語を解釈し始めるかもしれないが，通常の意味を確定するにあたっては，辞書だけでは必ずしも

---

(16) Report of the Appellate Body, United States - Countervailing Duty Investigation on Dynamic Random Access Memory Semiconductors (Drams) from Korea, WT/DS296/AB/R, 27 June 2005, at 5, para.12.

(17) Report of the Appellate Body, United States - Measures Relating to Shrimp from Thailand, United States -Customs Bond Directive for Merchandise Subject to Anti-Dumping/Countervailing Duties, WT/DS343/AB/R; WT/DS345/AB/R, 16 July 2008, at 60f., para.166.

(18) Report Of The Appellate Body, supra note 49, at 18f., para.38-40.

複雑な解釈問題を解決できるものではない．というのは，辞書はただ用語のすべての意味を並べるだけだからである．辞書は，条約の用語の意味を解釈する重要な指針であって，最終的な解釈を述べたものではない……．ウィーン条約法条約 31 条によると，条約用語の通常の意味は文脈により且つその趣旨及び目的に照らして確定されるべきである．……ウィーン条約法条約 31 条に定められた国際法上の慣習的規則による解釈は全体的解釈方法であり，機械的に硬直的な部分的作業に細分化されるべきではない．」そして，パネルが “sound recording distribution services” の意味を確定するために最も関連する辞書の定義を分析した際，なぜそれらの定義は他の定義より関連するのかについて言明をしなかったことについて，上級委員会は，「パネルの分析から見ると，中国が提出した定義も考えていたのであり，この点をはっきり説明しないから辞書の定義についての分析は間違っていた，とはいえないであろう．(19)」と述べて，パネルの判断を支持した．

この事件において，上級委員会は改めて，条約を解釈する際に，辞書の定義だけによって用語の意味を確定すべきではないことを強調した．

全体的に見ると，条約を解釈する際の辞書の利用について，上級委員会は全体的アプローチを強調している．つまり，通常の意味を

(19) “In its analysis of dictionary definitions for purposes of discerning the ordinary meaning of the term ‘Sound recording distribution services’, the Panel identified some meanings as more relevant to its analysis, but did not clearly explain why certain definitions were more relevant than others. However, we do not believe that the absence of a clear explanation amounts to an error in the Panel’s analysis of dictionary definitions, because its analysis makes clear that it took into consideration the meaning advocated by China, regardless of the dictionary sources of the various definitions before it.”
Id. at 148f., paras.356, 357.

判断するとき，辞書だけではなく，他の解釈のために参考にできる要素も考慮すべきだ，ということである．

ところが，異なる要素によって条約を解釈すると矛盾が生じる場合，「通常の意味」自身が曖昧であるから，実はこの矛盾は「全体的アプローチ」だけでは解決できないのである．その結果，上級委員会が辞書だけによって用語の通常の意味を判断すべきではないと何度強調しても，実際の紛争事件においては，辞書の利用についての論争が続いている．上級委員会の報告書から見れば，紛争事件における辞書の利用はまだコントロールされているが，パネル報告書について見れば，辞書の利用はすでに混乱状態に陥っている（既述）．

2 「国際紛争処理誌」における辞書の利用についての論争

⑴　論争の概要

2010年7月，台湾国立大学法学院のChang-Fa Lo教授は，オックスフォード大学出版局の国際紛争処理誌（the Journal of International Dispute Settlement）で“Good Faith Use of Dictionary in the Search of Ordinary Meaning under the WTO Dispute Settlement Understanding”という論文を発表した（本書冒頭参照）．Lo教授は，辞書の利用の原因を分析し，上級委員会が報告書の中で表明した辞書の利用についての意見をまとめた後，辞書の利用について8つのルールを提示した．2011年の1月，Lo教授のこの論文に対して，Isabelle Van Damme博士が，Lo教授の論文は辞書をなぜ利用すべきかを議論するものではなく辞書をどう利用すべきかを議論するものである[20]，またLo教授は辞書の利用を重視しすぎて，文脈，趣旨及び目的，当事国の後の合意，後に生じた慣行，他の国際法条約，条約締結の準備作業等，全体的アプローチ

⒇　Van Damme, supra note 2, at 235.

(holistic approach）の他の要素を軽視している[21]，として，同じ雑誌で，論文を発表して，Lo 教授に反論した．Isabelle Van Damme 博士の意見に対して Lo 教授は，2011 年の 7 月，再度，国際紛争処理誌で論文を通して，通常の意味と条約の趣旨及び目的を明らかにすることが条約解釈の第一歩であり，全体的アプローチはその後の第二ステップであると主張し，自己が提示した 8 つのルールは全体的アプローチを補充するものであり，全体的アプローチと条約解釈の柔軟性には影響を及ぼさない，と言明した[22]．ここでまず指摘すべきなのは，上級委員会の意見によると，条約用語の通常の意味も文脈により且つその趣旨及び目的に照らして確定されるべきであること，つまり，用語の通常の意味の確定は，条約の全体的解釈方法の不可分の一部分をなすこと，である．「通常の意味と条約の趣旨及び目的を明らかにするのが条約解釈の第一歩であり，全体的解釈方法はその後の第二ステップである」という Lo 教授の考え方は，まさに上級委員会が述べたように，条約解釈を「機械的に硬直的な部分的作業に細分化する」ことでしかないであろう．

(2) 8 つのルール[23]

以下では Lo 教授が提示した 8 つのルールを 1 つずつ検討する．

1) 解釈される条約と同じ言語の辞書のみを使うべきである．なぜなら，条約を交渉するとき，交渉に参加していた国の頭にある条約用語の意味は条約に使われる言語の意味だからである．用語の通常の意味を確定するために用語を他の言語に翻訳し，翻訳後の言語の辞書を用いるのは，適切とは言えない[24]．

---

(21) Id. at 233.

(22) Lo, Supra note 3, at 1.

(23) Lo, Supra note 1, at 443ff.

(24) “The language of the dictionary: The first principle should be to rely

Lo 教授のこの意見は，一見するとわかりやすいものだが，よく考えるとわからなくなる．「交渉に参加していた国の頭にある条約用語の言語」とは何の言語だろうか．例えば，WTO の場合，条約を締結する時に署名されたのは英語 ，フランス語，スペイン語の3つの言語の正文がある文書だが，そのうち，どの言語が「交渉に参加していた国の頭にある条約用語の言語」なのか．もし米国が締約国である場合に「交渉に参加していた国の頭にある条約用語の言語」が英語であると考えるならば，中国が締約国である場合はどうなるのか．ここで，締約国が署名したのはこの3つの言語の正文が同時に存在する文書であることに，注意すべきである．そして Lo 教授は，「WTO の公用語は英語，フランス語，スペイン語であるけれども，基本的には全てのパネルと上級委員会の報告書は英語で作成されている．その結果として，WTO 協定に出てくる用語の通常の意味を確定する目的でパネルや上級委員会が用いる辞書は，ほぼ英語のもののみであった.」と主張する(25)．ところが，そうすべきことの理由は，ないように思われる．「パネルと上級委員会が通常英語で報告書を書くこと」と「解釈の対象となる条約の用語の言

---

only on the dictionary with the same language of the treaty to be interpreted. Since when the negotiators negotiated an agreement, the meaning of a treaty term in their mind would be that of the language used for the agreement. It would not be appropriate to translate a treaty term into another language and use a dictionary of the other language to find out the ordinary meaning. Although the official languages of the WTO include English, French and Spanish, basically all panel and AB reports were drafted in English, and as a result virtually only English dictionaries were used by panels and the AB for the purpose of searching for the ordinary meanings of the terms in the WTO agreements."

Id. at 443.

(25) Ibid.

語」とは，どんな関係にあるのか．私は，紛争事件が生じる場合に，もし辞書の利用が必要であれば，最も関係がある言語の辞書を利用すべきであると思っている．もし紛争の当事国が全て英語圏の国々であれば，当然英語の条約の正文を基礎として議論すべきであるから，英語の辞書を利用することは自然である．もし当事国に英語圏の国とスペイン語圏の国の双方がある場合，英語の辞書とスペイン語の辞書のどちらを利用することも認められるはずである(26)．また，当事国の中で１カ国がこの３つの正式言語以外の言語の国である場合，いずれの言語の条約の正文も議論の基礎とすることは可能であるから，議論する条約の言語によって辞書を選ぶべきである．

2) 用語の性質によって，条約における用語の定義と用法に矛盾しない限り，専門辞書の意味も適用され得る．

この点については，パネルも同じ意見を表明した．EU による IT 製品の関税上の取扱事件において，当事国は，EU の約束表にある項目の用語について様々な辞書を利用した（表 3 参照）．パネルは「申立国は，約束表の項目の意味及び範囲について議論する際，約束表にある関係する用語の技術的辞書及びより一般的な英語の辞書における意味を利用した．用語を考えると，それは適当である.」と指摘した(27)．ところが，これはある場面では専門辞書の利用が認められるということを示しただけであり，いつ，どんな専門

(26) 菊地正・前掲第Ⅱ章注(53)239 頁.

(27) “The Panel notes that in their arguments about the meaning and scope of the concession at issue, the complainants have relied on various dictionary definitions of the relevant terms of the concession including technical dictionaries as well as more general dictionaries of the English language. Given the terms involved, we are of the view that this is appropriate.” Report of the Panel, supra note 36, at 221, para.7.468

辞書を利用すべきかに関する指導的ルールではないのである．

3）利用する辞書は形式的に限定されるべきではない．

従来は，パネルや上級委員会が利用する辞書の形式について，何の意見も示されていなかった．その結果，既に述べたように，紛争事件においてはCD-ROM，オンライン辞書，また誰でも随時書き込むことができるWikipedia等の電子版の辞書もよく使われた．情報技術の発展につれてこの傾向はますます強まっている．ところがここで改めて強調したいのは，オンライン辞書がいつの時点の意味を記載しているのかが不明確なことである．電子版の辞書と言っても，実は様々な種類がある．CD-ROMもあれば，オンライン辞書もある．また，オンライン辞書の中には，用語の意味の後に「何年何の版の辞書による」など出所がついている紙版の辞書と同じようなものもあるが，何もついていないものも多い．後者の場合，用語の意味がいつの時点のものなのか，不明確である．つまり，今あるオンライン辞書にある用語の意味が書いてあっても，それがいつの時点でこの用語の通常の意味であるかは，わからないのである．また，電子辞書には１つの重要な特徴，しかも紙版の辞書にはない特徴がある．それは更新スピードである．Wikipediaのような随時書き込むことができるオンライン辞書はその典型例であろう．電子版の辞書は，発達した情報技術によって，時代の要求に応じて次々と現れた新しい用語または用語の新しい用法を辞書に入れることができる一方，いつの時点の用語や意味を反映しているのかも曖昧になる．上級委員会は報告書の中で「条約解釈者の義務は，条約の用語を検討して締約国の意図を確定することである」[28]と指摘

---

(28) "The duty of a treaty interpreter is to examine the words of the treaty to determine the intentions of the parties."

Report of the Appellate Body, India - Patent Protection for Pharmaceutical and Agricultural Chemical Products , WT/DS50/AB/R, 19 De-

したが，時間的要素が曖昧であるオンライン辞書の意味によって，条約が締結された時の締約国の意図を確定することが，一体できるのか．アメリカ連邦最高裁判所の裁判官の中には，解釈の対象となる法律の制定と同時代の辞書を利用する方が，新しい意味を多く取り入れた新版の辞書を利用するよりも法律用語の意味を把握しやすいと考え，憲法や法令の解釈にあたってA New and Complete Law Dictionary（1771年版）やSamuel Johnson's Dictionary of the English Language（1773年版）を利用した者もいた[(29)]．

だが，実は，パネルや上級委員会は，この問題に気付いていた「かもしれない」のである．というのは，パネルや上級委員会の報告書の中で最も利用された辞書は，1993年版のThe New Shorter Oxford English Dictionaryだったからである．The New Shorter Oxford English Dictionaryは1990年版，1993年版，1996年版，1997年版，1999年版，2002年版，2003年版というように複数の版があるが，そのうち最も利用されたのは1993年版，すなわち1995年1月1日WTOの発足の日の前に一番近い版である．ところが，パネルや上級委員会がこの問題について何も説明していなかったため，実際の紛争事件においては，条約が締結された後に出版された辞書，最新の2009年版，2010年版の辞書，またオンライン辞書が，利用されることになってしまった．

4) 信用できる辞書を利用すべきである[(30)]．

情報技術の発展とともに，辞書の編集も容易になる．数えられないほど多くの辞書，特に大量のオンライン辞書の出現によって，どんな辞書が信用できるかという問題の重要性は高まっているのであ

cember 1997, at 18, para.45.

(29) Rubin, supra note 72, at 192 & 203; Kirchmeier / Thumma, supra note 82, at 97 & 113.

(30) Lo, supra note 1, at 444.

る．Lo 教授は，どんな辞書が信用できるかということを議論するにあたって，辞書の歴史，有名な出版社或いは有名な大学によって出版されているかどうか，出版の地域的範囲等の基準を示した．Isabelle Van Damme 博士は，出版社より出版物自身が有名であるかどうかが重要であると反論した[31]．前記の**表 4**（第Ⅱ章）を見ると，WTO 紛争処理事件で利用されたオックスフォード大学出版局の辞書の種類は様々であることが分かる．また，学生のための辞書，外国人のための辞書など他の様々な特定の読者のための辞書も含めれば，今までオックスフォード大学出版局によって出版された辞書は，数え切れないであろう．この中で，どれが信用できるのか，そう考えると，有名な出版社によって出版された有名な辞書は利用すべきである，と言うべきなのかもしれない．また，Wikipedia のような誰でも随時書き込むことができるオンライン辞書は，定義を書く人の身分や資格が全く分からない．信用できるかどうか疑問があるので，利用すべきではない，ということにもなるであろう．

5）　次に 5 番目と 6 番目のルールとして，Lo 教授は，異なる辞書の定義或いは同一の辞書の異なる定義について，ある定義を選ぶ理由をはっきり示さなければならない，と主張した．

中国の出版物及び音響映像製品の貿易権及び流通サービスに関する措置事件において，中国は上訴書で，「パネルが中国が提出した American Heritage Dictionary of the English Language（2000 年版）による“recording”の意味たる，『音声と映像を記録する媒体』(something on which sound or visual images have been recorded）を無視して，ごく一部の辞書だけによって結論を出したのは，あまりにもいい加減である．」と指摘したが，これに対して上級委員会は以下のように説明した．「パネルは “sound recording distri-

(31)　Van Damme, supra note 2, at 237.

bution services" の意味を確定するために最も関連する辞書の定義を分析したが，なぜそれらの定義が他の定義より関連性が深いのかを，説明しなかった．ところが，パネルの分析から見ると，中国が提出した定義も考慮していたと言えるので，はっきり説明していなくても，辞書の定義についての分析が間違いであったとはいえないであろう(32)」，と．また，上級委員会は，チリの農産物に対する価格拘束制度及びセーフガード措置事件の履行確認の上級委員会報告書の中で，「膨大な量の情報に対して，パネルは全ての証拠を分析，考慮し，結論の根拠とした証拠を示すべきであるが……レポートの中で，個々の証拠をどう扱ったのかをはっきり説明する必要はない.」という意見を提出した(33)．だが，紛争処理手続きによって安

(32) "In its analysis of dictionary definitions for purposes of discerning the ordinary meaning of the term "Sound recording distribution services", the Panel identified some meanings as more relevant to its analysis, but did not clearly explain why certain definitions were more relevant than others. However, we do not believe that the absence of a clear explanation amounts to an error in the Panel's analysis of dictionary definitions, because its analysis makes clear that it took into consideration the meaning advocated by China, regardless of the dictionary sources of the various definitions before it." Report of the Appellate Body, supra note 49, at 148f., paras.356,357.

(33) "We are mindful that the information placed before a panel is often voluminous in nature and that the probative value of specific pieces of evidence varies considerably. A panel must examine and consider all of the evidence placed before it, must identify the evidence upon which it has relied in reaching its findings, and must not make findings that are unsupported by evidence. Yet, a panel is also afforded a considerable margin of discretion in its appreciation of the evidence. This means, among other things, that a panel is not required, in its report, to explain precisely how it dealt with each and every piece of evidence on the panel record."

Report of the Appellate Body, Chile - Price Band System and Safe-

定性と予見可能性を提供することは，多角的体系であるWTOの目標と趣旨の達成を担保する要素である(34)．パネルはレポートの中で，個々の証拠をどう扱ったのかをはっきり説明する必要はないかもしれないが，問題となったのは，“sound recording distribution services”についてのパネルの判断が，パネルが選んだ辞書の定義に基づいてなされたこと，であった．つまり，辞書の定義は当該のパネルの判断の中で非常に重要な役割を果たしていたのである．この重要な判断の基礎の由来，つまり，なぜこれらの定義を選んだのかをはっきり説明しなければ，「安定性と予見可能性を提供する」という前記の基本的要請が空論に終わる可能性がある．パネルがこの点を説明しないのであれば，「結論の根拠となる証拠」を示さなかったと言えるであろう．

6)　最後の7・8番目のルールとして，Lo教授は，紛争事件において誰が辞書を利用することができるか，また辞書利用の形式の問題についての意見を表した．

Lo教授は，紛争事件においては当事国だけでなくパネルや上級委員会も，当事国によって提供された辞書の他，自ら選んだ辞書を利用することができる，と主張した(35)．パネルや上級委員会の報告書の中で，参照された紛争事件と同じように利用された辞書を列記することもまた，提案された(36)．

---

guard Measures Relating to Certain Agricultural Products Recourse to Article 21.5 of The DSU By Argentina, WT/DS207/AB/RW, 7 May 2007, at 86f., para.240.

(34)　Lo, supra note1, at 434及び佐分晴夫「WTOレジームの現段階――ケースを中心として――」日本国際経済法学会年報第8号（法律文化社，1999年）7，8頁.

(35)　Lo, supra note 1, at 444.

(36)　Id. at 445.

以上の8つのルールを見ると，Lo 教授は主に辞書をどう利用すべきかについて，意見を提示したと言える．ところが，既に述べたように，辞書の範囲を限定して「辞書の利用」を規律しようとすることには，様々な実際上の困難があって，境目を引くのは極めて困難である．また，辞書を利用したときに辞書と定義の選択理由が説明されても，「通常の意味」自身が曖昧であるので，異なる解釈要素によって選ばれた辞書の定義の対立も解決できないことになろう．上級委員会は，条約の用語の通常の意味を判断する際に辞書の定義だけによってそれを判断すべきではないことを強調したが，実はそれも Lo 教授の意見と同じで，辞書をどう利用すべきかについて述べたものであるにとどまる．他方，辞書を利用しすぎることと条約解釈における辞書定義の重要性の間には，一種の因果関係が存在している．条約用語の意味を判断する際に辞書が過度の重要性を与えられるからこそ，どうしても欲しい辞書の定義を見つけて，それを自らの主張の根拠とすることも出てくるのである．Lo 教授のルールによれば，ある程度辞書の利用を規律することができるのかもしれないが，条約の用語の意味を確定するにあたって辞書の定義に決定的な重要性がある状況が，今後も続いていけば，辞書の過度の利用もまた，避けられないものとなろう．

おわりに

本書では，WTO 紛争事件における辞書の利用の全体像及び辞書の利用についてのいくつかの論争の実例を見た上で，辞書の利用に対する上級委員会の見解や専門家の意見とアドバイス等も分析した．

上級委員会が米国ーガソリン基準事件で辞書を利用して以来，辞書が WTO 紛争処理事件で頻繁に利用され，条約解釈の際に重要な役割を果たすようになった．ところが，辞書が頻繁に利用される一方，紛争処理における議論で辞書の利用自体が論争の焦点になることも，多くなった．この問題について，本書は，上級委員会と Lo 教授の見解を，とくに重視して分析した．それらの見解は，主に辞書をどう利用すべきかについてのものである．ところが，ウィーン条約法条約 31 条と 32 条の規則によって条約解釈の中心になるはずの，「通常の意味」自体が曖昧であるから，「通常の意味」を判断するときの辞書の解釈の役割と重要性も，不明確となる．それに加えて，上級委員会と Lo 教授の見解は，辞書をなぜ利用すべきかについて触れることなく，辞書の利用を認めることを前提に，辞書をいかに利用すべきかについて述べたものである．ここで疑問となるのは，なぜ条約締結の準備作業などの解釈要素によって当事国の意思が既に明確である場合にも辞書の利用が必要であるのか，ということである．

それでは，辞書の利用に過度の重要性が与えられる原因は，何であろうか．よく考えると，それは単なる文言重視，ということではないだろうか．条約の文言を重視しているから，たとえ準備作業などの材料によって当事国の意思が既に明確であっても，文言と結びつけなければならないこととなり，そのために辞書が利用されるようになった．さらに，よく考えると，文言重視の裏には，実は一種の無力感が隠されているのではないか.

世界貿易機関を設立するマラケシュ協定の9条2項は,「閣僚会議及び一般理事会は,この協定及び多角的貿易協定の解釈を採択する排他的権限を有する」と定めている[(1)]. つまり,WTOの協定に対して排他的権限を以て解釈ができるのは,閣僚会議及び一般理事会である. ところが,9条2項は「解釈を採択する決定は,加盟国の4分の3以上の多数による議決で行う」とも定めている. WTOの加盟国が多いので,加盟国の意見が一致することは難しい. その結果,閣僚会議及び一般理事会による条約の解釈は余り実現できないことになる[(2)]. そこで,WTO協定を解釈するのは,実際はパネルや上級委員会である. DSU19条2項は,「パネル及び上級委員会は,第3条2項の規定に従うものとし,その認定及び勧告において,対象協定に定める権利及び義務に新たな権利及び義務を追加し,又は対象協定に定める権利及び義務を減ずることはできない」と定めているが,条約の中には,条約の締結を達成するために,起草する際にあえて曖昧にしておくところ,或いは実際に明らかにしていなかったところが,よくある[(3)]. これらの点については,もともと締約国の共同の意図がないかもしれないのである[(4)]. ところが,閣

(1) 条約邦訳は,小寺彰=中川淳司編・前掲第I章注(15) 3頁参照.

(2) Isabelle Van Damme, Treaty Interpretation by the WTO Appellate Body, Eur. J. Int. Law (2010) 21 (3), at 611.

(3) 「一般的に,法律を考えたときに,すべての事態を見通すように作ることは不可能である. 従って,法律は類似の場合に,より普遍的に適用されることを念頭において作られるが,それには,条文はある程度,多義的であることが必要である.」土屋裕明「多数国間条約に対する解釈宣言と条約の解釈」国際関係論研究(1996年10月号)33頁. 山形英郎「条約の解釈とは何か」法学セミナー(2010年1月号)19頁. 山形英郎「条約解釈目的と条約解釈手段―条約解釈規則の誕生―」法学雑誌(大阪市立大学)56巻3・4号(2010年3月)453頁.

(4) 土屋・前掲注(3)34頁,山手治之「条約の解釈」立命館法学48巻(1962

僚会議及び一般理事会による条約の解釈は実行できないから，これらの点についての解釈も，実際上，パネル及び上級委員会の役割となる．条約の文言によって当事国の共同の意図を常に判断することはできないから，パネル及び上級委員会が条約の文言を独立のものとして，重視し，そして，それに基づいて条約を解釈することもやむを得ないであろう．

そう考えると，紛争処理手続きにおける「辞書の利用」についての論争の裏には，様々な条約解釈，さらには条約の改正にかかわる問題が，隠されていることになる．だが，これらの問題についての検討は，今後の課題としたい．

年）107 頁，等参照．

資料1　WTOパネル報告書において利用された辞書一覧[1]

WT/DS8/R, WT/DS10/R, WT/DS11/R

The Shorter Oxford Dictionary

The Concise Oxford Dictionary of Current English

The American Heritage Dictionary, 2nd edition

WT/DS18/R

The New Shorter Oxford English Dictionary on Historical Principles, Vol. 2 (Clarendon Press, 1993)

WT/DS27/R

American Heritage Dictionary of the English language

WT/DS33/R

Webster's Encyclopedic Unabridged Dictionary of the English Language (1989)

WT/DS34/R

Webster's, New Twentieth Century Dictionary, unabridged, 2nd edition

WT/DS44/R

The Concise Oxford Dictionary (Ninth Edition 1995)

WT/DS46/R

Webster's Third International Dictionary

Webster's Third New International Dictionary of the English Language

The Concise Oxford Dictionary of the English Language

Shorter Oxford English Dictionary (third edition)

The Concise Oxford Dictionary of Current English, J.B. Sykes, Ed.

---

(1)　実際の報告書において引用された辞書のスタイルをあえてそのまま示す。

(Oxford: Clarendon Press, 1982)

Black's Law Dictionary (St. Paul: West Publishing Co., 6th ed.; 1990)

WT/DS48/R

The Concise Oxford Dictionary of Current English 8[a] ed.

Oxford English Dictionary

WT/DS50/R

The Oxford English Dictionary (Second Edition 1989)

WT/DS54/R, WT/DS55/R, WT/DS59/R, WT/DS64/R

Webster's Third New International Dictionary

The Compact Oxford English Dictionary (2d ed. 1987)

WT/DS56/R

Black's Law Dictionary, 6[a] edition, West Publishing (1991)

WT/DS69/R

The Oxford English Dictionary

WT/DS70/R

Black's Law Dictionary

Webster's Third New International Dictionary of the English Language

The New Shorter Oxford English Dictionary on Historical Principles, Vol. 1 (Oxford: Clarendon Press, 1993)

Robert & Collins French-English Dictionary (Paris & London: Dictionnaires Le Robert and Collins Publishers, 1987)

The Oxford Encyclopedic English Dictionary (Oxford University Press: Oxford, 1991)

WT/DS75/R, WT/DS84/R

Webster's dictionary

The Shorter Oxford English Dictionary

The New Shorter Oxford English Dictionary (Clarendon Press, 1993)

WT/DS76/R

Webster's Encyclopedic Unabridged Dictionary of the English Language, 1996 Random House

A Dictionary of the Flowering Plants and Ferns, Cambridge University Press (1960)

WT/DS79/R

Black's Law Dictionary (Sixth Edition)

WT/DS90/R

New Oxford Shorter English Dictionary (1993)

Webster's New Encyclopedic Dictionary (1993)

WT/DS98/R

The New Webster Encyclopedic Dictionary

The New Shorter Oxford Dictionary

WT/DS99/R

Webster's II New Riverside University Dictionary (1984)

Black's Law Dictionary, 6th ed. (West Publishing Co., 1990)

WT/DS103/R, WT/DS113/R

The Oxford English Dictionary (2nd Edition) - Volume XI, Clarendon Press, 1989

The Dictionary of Canadian Law (Toronto, 1991)

The New Shorter Oxford English Dictionary (Ed. Brown, L., Clarendon Press, Oxford)

The New Shorter Oxford English Dictionary on Historical Principles, Lesley Brown (ed.), (Oxford: Oxford University Press, 1993)

Webster's II, New Riverside University Dictionary, 1994

Black's Law Dictionary, 6th ed., (West Publishing Co.: Minneapolis Minn., 1990)

WT/DS108/R

The New Shorter Oxford English Dictionary (1993)

Webster's Third New International Dictionary (1976)

Webster's Third New International Dictionary of the English Language Unabridged, G. & C. Merriam (1961)

Concise Oxford Dictionary, Ninth edition, 1995

Shorter Oxford English Dictionary (Third Edition)

Black's Law Dictionary (Revised fourth edition)

Webster's Third International Dictionary

WT/DS114/R

Black's Law Dictionary

The New Shorter Oxford English Dictionary, Lesley Brown (ed.) (1993)

Oxford Dictionary

The Shorter Oxford English Dictionary

Diccionario de la Lengua Española, Real Academia de la Lengua, 1956

WT/DS121/R

The New Shorter Oxford English Dictionary on Historical Principles, Oxford (1993)

WT/DS122/R

Concise Oxford Dictionary (1990 ed.)

Oxford English Dictionary (1971)

The New Shorter Oxford English Dictionary (1993 ed.)

Webster's Ninth New Collegiate Dictionary (1990)

The Shorter Oxford English Dictionary (1973)

Webster's Ninth New Collegiate Dictionary (Merriam-Webster 1996)

WT/DS126/R

The Concise Oxford Dictionary, 8th ed., Clarendon Press

Shorter Oxford English Dictionary, third ed.

Concise Oxford Dictionary, ninth ed., 1995

The New Shorter Oxford English Dictionary, 1993

WT/DS132/R

Concise Oxford Dictionary, 1976

WT/DS135/R

Petit Robert 1, Dictionary of the French language

Dictionnaire Robert, (Robert French Dictionary), 1993 edition

Larousse French dictionary

The Shorter Oxford English Dictionary on Historical Principles, Oxford, 1993

Black's Law Dictionary (1990)

The New Shorter Oxford English Dictionary (1993)

WT/DS136/R

The New Shorter Oxford English Dictionary (1993)

Black's Law Dictionary, 6th Ed. (1990)

WT/DS138/R

The Oxford English Dictionary (Oxford University Press 1971)

Black's Law Dictionary, West Publishing Co. (6th Ed. 1990)

The 1993 New Shorter Oxford English Dictionary

WT/DS139/R, WT/DS142/R

Webster's New World Dictionary, Third College Edition

The New Shorter Oxford English Dictionary on Historical Principles (Oxford: Clarendon Press, 1993)

Merriam-Webster's Collegiate Dictionary (10th ed. [Markham: Thomas Allen, 1993])

The Concise Oxford Dictionary of Current English, 8th Edition (Clarendon Press: Oxford, 1990)

The Concise Oxford Dictionary of Current English (Oxford: Clarendon Press, 1995)

Black's Law Dictionary (West Publishing Co., 1968, Fourth Edition)

WT/DS141/R

The New Shorter Oxford English Dictionary, Clarendon Press, Oxford, 1993

Webster's New Collegiate Dictionary, 1975

Webster's II New Riverside Dictionary, 1984

The Concise Oxford Dictionary of Current English

Oxford Student's Dictionary

Webster's New World Dictionary, 3rd College Edition 1994

Webster's dictionary

The New Shorter Oxford Dictionary (1996)

WT/DS142/R

Dictionnaire alphabetique et analogique de la Langue Francaise Paul Robert, 1964

WT/DS146/R, WT/DS175/R

The New Shorter Oxford Dictionary

Webster's New World Dictionary, Third College Edition

Black's Law Dictionary

Webster's New Encyclopedic Dictionary, 1994

WT/DS152/R

The Oxford English Dictionary

Oxford English Reference Dictionary

Black's Law Dictionary, Revised 4th edition (West Publishing Co., 1968)

Black's Law Dictionary, 5th ed.

Black's Law Dictionary (Sixth Edition)

WT/DS155/R

Webster's New World Dictionary, Third College Edition

Black's Law Dictionary. Revised Fourth Edition, 1968

The New Shorter Oxford English Dictionary, Vol. II, Oxford (1993)

WT/DS156/R

The Compact Edition of the Oxford English Dictionary (Oxford University Press 1971)

Webster's Encyclopedic Unabridged Dictionary of the English Language (Gramercy Books, 1994)

The New Shorter Oxford English Dictionary, Oxford University Press, 1993

The Concise Oxford English Dictionary, Clarendon Press, 1995

Diccionario de la Lengua Española, Twenty-First Edition (Real Academia Española, 1992)

Diccionario Larousse, 1987 Edition

WT/DS160/R

The New Shorter Oxford English Dictionary (1993)

Oxford English Dictionary

WT/DS161/R, WT/DS169/R

The New Shorter Oxford English Dictionary (1993 ed.)

Collins Concise Dictionary, William Collins and Son

WT/DS162/R

The New Shorter Oxford English Dictionary (1993)

Black's Law Dictionary, 6th Ed. (1990)

WT/DS163/R

The New Shorter Oxford English Dictionary (1993 ed.)

Black's Law Dictionary (6th ed., 1990)

WT/DS165/R

Webster New Encyclopedic Dictionary

The New Shorter Oxford English Dictionary

The New Little Oxford Dictionary

Black Law Dictionary (6th Ed.)

WT/DS166/R

The Oxford dictionary

Webster's New 3d Int'l Dictionary (1981).
The New Webster Encyclopedic Dictionary
The New Shorter Oxford Dictionary
Oxford English Reference Dictionary, Oxford University Press, 1995
The Concise Oxford Dictionary

WT/DS170/R

The Concise Oxford Dictionary of Current English, Seventh Edition (Oxford: The Clarendon Press, 1982)
The New Oxford Dictionary of English (Oxford University Press, 1998)
Webster's New World Dictionary (The World Publishing Company, 1976)
Black's Law Dictionary (West Publishing Co., 1979)
The New Shorter Oxford English Dictionary (1993)

WT/DS174/R

The New Shorter Oxford English Dictionary (1993)
Diccionario de la lengua Española

WT/DS176/R

The New Shorter Oxford English Dictionary (Clarendon Press, 1993)
The New Oxford Dictionary of English (Oxford University Press, 1998)
Black's Law Dictionary (West Publishing Co., Fifth Edition)
Diccionario de Ciencias Juridicas, Politicas y Sociales (1984)

WT/DS177/R, WT/DS178/R

Oxford English Dictionary
Webster's New Encyclopedic Dictionary (1994)
NSOED - New Shorter Oxford English Dictionary CD version, January 1997
A Dictionary of Modern Legal usage: Bryan A. Garner, Oxford University Press 1987
The New Shorter Oxford English Dictionary (1993)

Webster's Third New International Dictionary (1981)

Webster's New Collegiate Dictionary (1977)

Webster's Ninth New Collegiate Dictionary (1985)

WT/DS179/R

New Shorter Oxford English Dictionary, Oxford University Press, 1993

Webster's Third New International Dictionary

Webster's II New Riverside University Dictionary (1984)

WT/DS184/R

New Shorter Oxford English Dictionary, Clarendon Press, Oxford, 1993

Concise Oxford Dictionary, ninth edition, Clarendon Press, Oxford, 1995

Black's Law Dictionary, 7th ed. (1999)

Black's Law Dictionary (6th ed. 1990)

Webster's Third New International Dictionary (1981)

The Compact Edition of the Oxford English Dictionary (1971)

The Compact Edition of the Oxford English Dictionary (1985)

WT/DS189/R

Black's Law Dictionary

Webster's New World Dictionary (Third College Edition)

The New Shorter Oxford English Dictionary (Clarendon Press Oxford, 1993)

WT/DS192/R

The New Shorter Oxford English Dictionary

Fairchild's Dictionary of Textiles (7th ed., 1996)

The Concise Oxford Dictionary, Third Edition, Oxford at the Clarendon Press

Dictionary of Fibre & Textile Technology (1990)

Webster's New Encyclopedic Dictionary

WT/DS194/R

The New Shorter Oxford English Dictionary (Oxford: Clarendon Press, 1993)

The Concise Oxford Dictionary, Ninth Edition, 1995, Clarendon Press, Oxford

Merriam-Webster's Collegiate Dictionary, 10th ed. (Springfield, Mass.: Merriam-Webster, 1993)

WT/DS202/R

Dictionary of International Trade Terms (William S. Hein & Co., Inc. 1996)

The Compact Edition of the Oxford English Dictionary, Volume 1 (Oxford University Press, 1971)

WT/DS204/R

Black's Law Dictionary, 6th edition, 1990

Newton's Telecom Dictionary, 19th Edition, March 2000

The Shorter Oxford English Dictionary, 3rd edition (Clarendon Press, 1990)

Merriam Webster Online Dictionary, at http://www.webster.com/cgi-bin/dictionary. 2003

The New Shorter Oxford English Dictionary (Clarendon Press, 1993)

Black's Law Dictionary (West Publishing, 1995)

WT/DS206/R

The New Shorter Oxford English Dictionary, Clarendon Press, Oxford, 1993

Oxford Standard Dictionary

The Concise Oxford English Dictionary, Clarendon Press, 1995

Harcourt, Academic Dictionary of Science and Technology, at http://www.harcourt.com/dictionary/browse

WT/DS207/R

Dictionary of Trade Policy Terms (Centre for International Economic Studies, University of Adelaide, 1997)

Robert Collins French English, English French Dictionary (Beverly T. Atkins et al., 2nd ed. 1987)

The Oxford Spanish Dictionary (Beatriz Galimberti Jarman et al., eds., 1994)

The Oxford English Dictionary (2d edition)

The New Shorter Oxford English Dictionary

Webster's Encyclopaedic English Dictionary

Collins Spanish-English Dictionary, 14th edition

Le Petit Robert Dictionnaire de la Langue Française (J. Rey-Debove and A. Rey, Eds.), 2nd edition

WT/DS211/R

Oxford English Dictionary Online, at http://dictionary.oed.com

Merriam-Webster's Collegiate Dictionary online, at http://www.m-w.com

The Concise Oxford Dictionary (10th ed.)

The Shorter Oxford English Dictionary, 1993

Webster's New World Dictionary, 2nd College Edition, 1986

Black's Law Dictionary, Revised 4th Edition

WT/DS213/R

New Shorter Oxford English Dictionary

Oxford Concise English Dictionary, 9th ed. 1995

American Heritage Dictionary (3rd ed. 1994)

Merriam-Webster's Dictionary of Law

WT/DS217/R, WT/DS234/R

The New Shorter Oxford English Dictionary, Vol. 2 (Oxford: Clarendon Press, 1993)

The Oxford English Dictionary Online (www.oed.com)

The Webster's Encyclopedic Unabridged Dictionary

WT/DS219/R

The New Shorter Oxford English Dictionary, Clarendon Press, Oxford, 1993

Oxford English Dictionary Online, at http://dictionary.oed.com

Oxford English Encyclopedic Dictionary (1991)

Webster's New Encyclopedic Dictionary (1994)

Merriam-Webster's Collegiate Dictionary online, at http://www.m-w.com

Webster's New World Dictionary

Concise Oxford Dictionary

WT/DS221/R

The New Shorter Oxford English Dictionary, Clarendon Press, Oxford, 1993

WT/DS222/R

The New Shorter Oxford English Dictionary, Clarendon Press, Oxford, 1993

Walter Goode, Dictionary of Trade Policy Terms, Centre for International Economic Studies, University of Adelaide, 2nd ed., 1998

Black's Law Dictionary, 5th Ed. (1979)

A Dictionary of Accounting, (Oxford: University Press, 1999), available online at www.xrefer.com

WT/DS231/R

European Communities Multilingual Dictionary

The Multilingual Dictionary of Fish and Fish Products prepared by the Organization for Economic Cooperation and Development (OECD)

Multilingual Illustrated Dictionary of Aquatic Animals and Plants

Oxford Dictionary

The Grand Dictionnaire Encyclopédique Larousse

Diccionario de la lengua española

The New Shorter Oxford English Dictionary, Clarendon Press, Oxford, 1993

The Cassell Thesaurus Dictionary (Mackays of Chatham PLC, 1998)

Black's Law Dictionary (West Publishing Company, 1979, fifth edition)

The New Oxford Dictionary of English (Clarendon Press, Oxford, 1998)

Webster's New World Dictionary (William Collins & World Publishing Co., Inc., 1976)

WT/DS236/R

New Shorter Oxford English Dictionary (Oxford: Clarendon Press, 1993)

Black's Law Dictionary, 7th ed. (St. Paul: West, 1999)

The Concise Oxford Dictionary of Current English, 8th ed. (Oxford: Clarendon Press, 1990)

The Concise Oxford Dictionary, ninth edition, Clarendon Press

Webster's Ninth New Collegiate Dictionary (Markham: Merriam-Webster, 1991)

WT/DS238/R

The Dictionary of the Real Academia Española de la Lengua

WT/DS241/R

Black's Law Dictionary (West Publishing Co., 1990)

The Concise Oxford Dictionary of Current English (Clarendon Press, 1995)

The New Shorter Oxford English Dictionary (Clarendon Press, 1993)

The Dictionary of the Real Academia Española

The Concise Oxford Dictionary – Ninth Edition, Oxford University

Press, 1995

WT/DS243/R

The New Shorter Oxford English Dictionary, L. Brown (ed.) (Clarendon Press, 1993)

Fairchild's Dictionary of Textiles, Fairchild Publications, Inc., New York, 1970

The Dictionary of Economics (edited by John Eatwell and published in 1987 by Macmillan Press)

The New Oxford Thesaurus of English

Black's Law Dictionary, B. A. Garner (ed.), West Group, 1999

WT/DS244/R

Oxford English Encyclopedic Dictionary (1991)

Webster's New Universal Unabridged Dictionary, 2nd Ed. (1983)

Black's Law Dictionary (5th ed. West Group 1979)

The New Shorter Oxford English Dictionary (1993)

Webster's II New Riverside University Dictionary (1994)

WT/DS245/R

The New Shorter Oxford English Dictionary, vol. 1, Oxford University Press, 1993

WT/DS246/R

The New Shorter Oxford English Dictionary, 4th Edition

The New Shorter Oxford English Dictionary, L. Brown (ed.) (Clarendon Press, 1993)

Black's Law Dictionary, 7th ed., B.A. Garner (ed.) (West Group, 1999)

The Concise Oxford Dictionary of Current English, 7th Edition

Webster's New World Dictionary (2nd Concise ed. 1982)

WT/DS248/R, WT/DS249/R, WT/DS251/R, WT/DS252/R, WT/DS253/R, WT/DS254/R, WT/DS258/R, WT/DS259/R

New Shorter Oxford English Dictionary (1993)
Webster's Third New International Dictionary
The Oxford English Dictionary
The New Shorter Oxford English Dictionary (electronic version) January 1997

WT/DS257/R

The New Shorter Oxford English Dictionary, 1993
Black's Law Dictionary, 7th edition, 1999
Le nouveau Petit Robert, 1998
Diccionario de uso del Español, 1988
Concise Oxford Dictionary, Ninth Edition
Webster's New World Dictionary, Third College Edition
Harrap's Shorter French – English Dictionary, Chambers Harrap Publishers Ltd, 1996

WT/DS264/R

The Concise Oxford Dictionary of Current English (Clarendon Press, 1995)
The New Shorter Oxford English Dictionary, 3rd ed. (Oxford: The Clarendon Press, 1993)
Joel G. Siegel and Jae K. Shim, Dictionary of Accounting Terms (Barron's Educational Services, Inc. 2nd ed. 1995)

WT/DS265/R, WT/DS266/R

Black's Law Dictionary, Sixth Edition, 1991
The New Shorter Oxford English Dictionary
Webster's New Encyclopedic Dictionary, 1994 ed.

WT/DS267/R

The New Shorter Oxford English Dictionary, (1993)
Concise Oxford English Dictionary (Oxford: Clarendon Press, 1995)
Webster's Revised Unabridged Dictionary (1996)

Dictionary of Economics (The Economist Books, 1999)
Dictionary of International Finance (The Economist Books, 1999)
Merriam-Webster Dictionary online

WT/DS268/R

New Shorter Oxford English Dictionary (1993)
Black's Law Dictionary (7th ed. West Group 1999)
Black's Law Dictionary (5th ed. 1979)
Webster's New Collegiate Dictionary (1979)
The New Oxford Dictionary of English
The American Heritage Dictionary (2d ed. 1982)
The American Heritage Dictionary of the English Language (3rd ed.)
Concise Oxford English Dictionary (10th ed. 2001)
Merriam-Webster Online Dictionary (2002)
Ballentine's Law Dictionary (3d ed. 1969)
The Random House Dictionary of the English Language (1966)
Webster's Third New Int'l Dictionary of the English Language (1981)

WT/DS269/R

Concise Oxford Dictionary (1995)
American Heritage College Dictionary (1993)
Merriam Webster's Collegiate Dictionary (1993)
New Shorter Oxford English Dictionary (1996)
Concise Oxford Dictionary (1999)
Webster's New Encyclopedic Dictionary (1993)
New Shorter Oxford English Dictionary (1993)
Black's Law Dictionary
Arnold Bender's Dictionary of Nutrition and Food Technology
Concise Oxford Dictionary (2001)
The Shorter Oxford English Dictionary on Historical Principles – Third Edition, Oxford at the Clarendon Press, 1944

WT/DS273/R

Webster's New Twentieth Century Dictionary, unabridged second edition

The New Shorter Oxford English Dictionary, Volume 1, 1993

Oxford English Dictionary

Random House Dictionary

WT/DS276/R

The New Shorter Oxford English Dictionary, L. Brown (ed.) (Clarendon Press, 1993)

Merriam-Webster's Collegiate Dictionary: Tenth Edition (2001)

Black's Law Dictionary (1979)

WT/DS277/R

The New Shorter Oxford English Dictionary, L. Brown (ed.) (Clarendon Press, 1993)

The Concise Oxford Dictionary

WT/DS282/R

New Shorter Oxford English Dictionary, Clarendon Press, Oxford, 1993

Webster's II New College Dictionary

WT/DS285/R

New Shorter Oxford English Dictionary (1993)

Shorter Oxford English Dictionary, 2002

Merriam-Webster's Collegiate Dictionary, (10th ed. 2001)

Merriam-Webster Dictionary Online, found at http://www.m-w.com/cgi-bin/dictionary

The Oxford English Dictionary (1938)

The Oxford English Dictionary (1986)

Collier's Dictionary, 1977

Chambers Online Reference, at http://.chambersharrap.co.uk/chambers/chref/chref.py/main

The American Heritage Dictionary, Online edition, at http://www.bartleby.com

The American Heritage Dictionary (4th ed., 2000)

Webster's Third New International Dictionary, 1986

The Random House Dictionary of the English Language, 2nd ed., 1987

Webster's II New Riverside University Dictionary, 1988

Encarta World English Dictionary, available at http://encarta.msn.com/dictionary_/sporting.html, 2004

Webster New Encyclopedic Dictionary, 1993

WT/DS290/R

A Supplement to the Oxford English Dictionary, R.W. Burchfield (ed.) (Clarendon Press, 1972, reprinted, with corrections, 1980)

The New Shorter Oxford English Dictionary (1993)

WT/DS291/R, WT/DS292/R, WT/DS293/R

The New Shorter Oxford English Dictionary, L. Brown (ed.) (Clarendon Press, 1993)

The Concise Oxford Dictionary, 10th ed., J. Pearsall (ed.) (Clarendon Press, 1999)

The New Shorter Oxford English Dictionary, L. Brown (ed.) (Clarendon Press, 2002)

Webster's New World Dictionary of American English, V. Neufeldt and D. B. Guralnik eds., New York, Simon & Schuster, 1993

The Penguin Pocket English Dictionary (1988)

The New Oxford Thesaurus of English

The New Little Oxford Dictionary, 1989

Dictionary of Trade Policy Terms (2nd ed.), Walter Goode, 1998

Http://www.biology-online.org/dictionary.asp

The Compact Oxford English Dictionary, Oxford University Press, 1971, 24th Printing

McGraw-Hill Dictionary of Scientific and Technical Terms, 6th ed.

Webster's New Encyclopedic Dictionary (Könemann, 1993)

Concise Oxford English Dictionary, Eleventh Ed. 2004

WT/DS294/R

The New Shorter Oxford English Dictionary

WT/DS295/R

New Shorter Oxford English Dictionary (1993)

WT/DS296/R

The New Shorter Oxford English Dictionary, Fourth Edition, Clarendon Press (1993)

The Concise Oxford Dictionary, Ninth Edition, Clarendon Press, Oxford (1995)

New Shorter Oxford English Dictionary (5th ed. 2002)

Oxford Hachette French Dictionary, Third Edition, Oxford University Press (2001)

Oxford Spanish Dictionary, Third Edition, Oxford University Press (2003)

WT/DS299/R

The New Shorter Oxford Dictionary, Third edition

The Concise Oxford Dictionary, Ninth edition

WT/DS301/R

The New Shorter Oxford English Dictionary (1993)

Webster New Encyclopedic Dictionary

WT/DS302/R

The New Shorter Oxford English Dictionary, Fourth Edition, Oxford University Press, 1993

Webster's New Encyclopedic Dictionary, 1994

資料1　WTOパネル報告書において利用された辞書一覧

WT/DS308/R

The New Shorter Oxford English Dictionary (Clarendon Press, 1993)

Black's Law Dictionary (1990)

WT/DS312/R

Concise Oxford English Dictionary, Tenth Edition

WT/DS315/R

The New Shorter Oxford English Dictionary (1993)

Collins Spanish Dictionary, 1985

Robert & Collins Senior, 2002

Black's Law Dictionary, 1999

Dictionary of International Trade, 2000

Merriam-Webster Online Dictionary, http://www.m-w.com/cgi-bin/dictionary

WT/DS320/R

Shorter Oxford English Dictionary, 5th edition (1993)

Webster Online Dictionary

Merriam-Webster Online Dictionary (http://www.m-w.com/dictionary/epidemiology)

Black Law Dictionary, 6th ed.

The New Shorter Oxford English Dictionary on Historical Principles (Clarendon Press, 1993)

The American Heritage Dictionary of the English Language (4th ed., 2000)

The Shorter Oxford English Dictionary, fifth ed., 2002

WT/DS321/R

Shorter Oxford English Dictionary, 5th edition (1993)

Webster Online Dictionary

Merriam-Webster Online Dictionary (http://www.m-w.com/dictionary/epidemiology)

Black Law Dictionary, 6th ed.

The New Shorter Oxford English Dictionary on Historical Principles (Clarendon Press, 1993)

The American Heritage Dictionary of the English Language (4th ed., 2000)

The Shorter Oxford English Dictionary (5th ed., 2002)

Dictionnaire de droit international public

Stedman's Medical Dictionary (2000)

Taber's Cyclopedic Medical Dictionary - 20th Ed (2005)

WT/DS322/R

New Shorter Oxford English Dictionary, 1993

WT/DS332/R

The Shorter Oxford English Dictionary, L. Brown (ed.) (Oxford University Press, 2002)

WT/DS334/R

Shorter Oxford English Dictionary, Fifth Edition, Oxford University Press, 2003

Osborne's Concise Law Dictionary, 8th ed. (Sweet & Maxwell, 1993)

Jowitt's Dictionary of English Law, 2nd ed. by J. Burke (Sweet & Maxwell, 1977)

The New Shorter Oxford English Dictionary (Clarendon Press, 1993)

WT/DS335/R

Collins English Dictionary 21st century edition (5th edition 2000)

WT/DS336/R

The New Shorter Oxford Dictionary

The Concise Oxford English Dictionary (10th ed. 2002)

The Oxford English Dictionary (2nd ed. 1989)

Shorter Oxford English Dictionary (5th ed. 2002)

WT/DS337/R

Shorter Oxford English Dictionary (fifth edition, 2002)

New Shorter Oxford English Dictionary, Clarendon Press, 1993

WT/DS341/R

The Shorter Oxford English Dictionary

The New Shorter Oxford Dictionary, 1993

Black's Law Dictionary, 7th Edition, abridged. (2000)

Webster's New Encyclopedic Dictionary, 2000

Le Grand Robert de la langue française

The Collins Spanish Dictionary (1985)

The Merriam-Webster dictionary (online edition)

The Dictionary of the Real Academia Español (online version)

The Dictionary of the Académie Française (online version)

The Dictionary of the Spanish Royal Academy of Language

WT/DS339/R, WT/DS340/R, WT/DS342/R

Dictionary of Trade Policy Terms, W. Goode, WTO Fourth Edition, 2003

The Shorter Oxford English Dictionary, 2002 (5th edition)

The New Shorter Oxford English Dictionary

WCO, Glossary of International Customs Terms, 2006

Webster's New Encyclopedic Dictionary, 2003

Le Grand Robert de la Langue Française

Black's Law Dictionary, Seventh Edition, 1999

Handbook of the Global Trade Community, Dictionary of International Trade, E. Hinkelman, Fourth Edition, 2000

The American Heritage College Dictionary, Third Edition (1993)

Dictionary of Automobile Engineering, Peter Collin Publishing, 1997

Diccionario de uso del Español 1987

WT/DS343/R

New Shorter Oxford dictionary, vol. 2 (1993)

Black's Law Dictionary, 7th ed., B.A. Garner (ed.) (West Group, 1999)

WT/DS345/R

Ballentine's Law Dictionary (West Publishing, 3d. ed.)

The New Shorter Oxford English Dictionary (Clarendon Press, 4th Ed. 1993)

WT/DS350/R

Shorter Oxford English Dictionary (Oxford University Press, 2002)

The New Shorter Oxford English Dictionary (1993)

WT/DS360/R

The New Shorter Oxford English Dictionary, L. Brown (ed.) (Clarendon Press), 1993

Shorter Oxford English Dictionary, 5th ed., W.R. Trumble, A. Stevenson (eds.) (Oxford University Press, 2002)

Merriam-Webster Online Dictionary, available at http://www.merriam-webster.com/-dictionary/equivalent

WT/DS362/R

New Shorter Oxford English Dictionary (1993)

The Shorter Oxford English Dictionary (Fifth edition, 2002)

WT/DS363/R

New Shorter Oxford English Dictionary, L. Brown (ed.) (Clarendon Press 1993)

Black's Law Dictionary, 8th ed., B.A. Garner (ed.) (West Group 2004)

Shorter Oxford English Dictionary, 5th ed. (Clarendon Press 2002)

Black's Law Dictionary, 7th ed., B.A. Garner (ed.) (West Group 1999)

American Heritage Dictionary, 4th ed. (Houghton Mifflin 2000), available at http://www.bartleby.com/61/

Oxford English Dictionary Online available at http://dictionary.oed.com/entrance.dtl)

The New Century Chinese English Dictionary

Shorter Oxford English Dictionary, 6th ed. (Clarendon Press 2007)

Businessdictionary.com

The Monash Marketing Dictionary, www.buesco.monash.edu.au/mkt/dictionary

Random House Unabridged Dictionary (Random House 1997) available at http://dictionary.infoplease.com/distribution

Webster's New Encyclopedic Dictionary (Black Dog & Leventhal 1993)

BNET Business Dictionary available at http://dictionary.bnet.com/definition/Distribution+Channel.html

WT/DS366/R

Shorter Oxford English Dictionary, 5th edition (2002)

Black's Law Dictionary, 7th edition (2000)

Shorter Oxford English Dictionary, 5th edition (1993)

The New Oxford Dictionary of English (Clarendon Press, 2nd Ed. 2001)

WT/DS367/R

The New Shorter Oxford English Dictionary (Clarendon Press, 1993)

The Oxford English Dictionary online, http://www.oed.com

WT/DS375/R, WT/DS376/R, WT/DS377/R

McGraw-Hill Dictionary of Scientific and Technical Terms, 1994 (fifth edition)

The 1993 and 2003 McGraw-Hill Dictionary of Scientific and Technical Terms

New Shorter Oxford English Dictionary, 1993 (4th edition)

New Shorter Oxford English Dictionary, fifth edition, 2002

New Shorter Oxford English Dictionary, fifth edition, 2003

Microsoft Computer Dictionary (5th ed., 2002)

Techweb On-line Dictionary, available at: http://www.techweb.com/encyclopedia/defineterm.jhtml?term=flatpaneldisplay

ITV Dictionary, http://www.itvdictionary.com

Newton's Telecom Dictionary (10th ed. 1996)

Newton's Telecom Dictionary (2004, 20th ed.)

Newton's Telecom Dictionary (24th Ed. 2008)

Yourdictionary.com, http://www.yourdictionary.com/set-top-box

Foldoc, Free Online Dictionary of Computing, http://foldoc.org/index.cgi?query=set+top+box

IEEE Standard Dictionary of Electrical and Electronics Terms (6th ed. 1996)

The Shorter Oxford Dictionary (1993)

The Shorter Oxford Dictionary (2002)

The Shorter Oxford Dictionary (2003)

Merriam-Webster online Dictionary

The Authoritative Dictionary of IEEE Standard Terms (2000)

Dictionary of Business Terms (3rd ed.)

Webster's New Encyclopedia Dictionary (1993)

Le nouveau Petit Robert (2000)

The Dictionary of Trade Policy Terms and the Dictionary of International Trade)

Oxford English Dictionary, 2nd ed. 1989 (emphasis added)

WT/DS379/R

Shorter Oxford English Dictionary, L. Brown (ed.) (Claredon Press, 1993)

Dictionary online, http://www.thefreedictionary.com.

Accurate and Reliable Dictionary online, <http://ardictionary.com/>

Free Dictionary online, <http://encyclopedia.thefreedictionary.com/Scottish+public+bodies>

Real Academia Española Dictionary online , <http://buscon.rae.es/draeI/>

The Oxford Spanish Dictionary, B. Galimberti (ed.) (Oxford University Press, 2003)

Spanish Dict online, <http://www.spanishdict.com/translate/perteneciente>

Investment Dictionary

Financial & Investment Dictionary and Business Dictionary:

Wikipedia

WT/DS383/R

Diccionario de la Lengua Española, Espasa Calpe, Madrid, 2005

WT/DS392/R

Merriam-Webster Online Dictionary, from http://www.merriam-webster.com/dictionary/approving

The New Shorter Oxford English Dictionary, Clarendon Press, 1993

Oxford English Dictionary Online

WT/DS397/R

New Shorter Oxford English Dictionary, Clarendon Press, 1993

WT/DS399/R

Shorter Oxford English Dictionary (2007 ed.)

Webster's Ninth New Collegiate Dictionary (1986 ed.)

Trésor de la Langue Francaise, dictionary published by the CNRS (National Center for Scientific Research), available at: http://atilf.atilf.fr/tlf.htm

Diccionario de la Lengua Espanola, dictionary published by the Real Academia Espanola, available at: http://www.rae.es/rae.html

The Oxford Spanish Dictionary (2003 ed.)

The New Shorter Oxford English Dictionary, (1993)

The Compact Edition of the Oxford English Dictionary (Oxford Uni-

versity Press, 1971)
Concise Oxford English Dictionary, tenth edition

資料2　WTO上級委員会報告書において利用された辞書一覧

WT/DS2/AB/R

The New Shorter Oxford English Dictionary on Historical Principles (L. Brown, ed., 1993)

WT/DS18/AB/R

The Concise Oxford Dictionary of Current English (9th ed., Clarendon Press)

WT/DS26/AB/R

The New Shorter Oxford English Dictionary on Historical Principles (1993)

WT/DS27/AB/R

A Dictionary of Modern Legal Usage (Oxford University Press, 1987)

A Dictionary of Law, 4th ed. (Pitman Publishing, 1993)

WT/DS33/AB/R

Osborne's Concise Law Dictionary, 8ª ed. (Sweet & Maxwell, 1993)

Jowitt's Dictionary of English Law, 2ª ed. a cargo de J. Burke (Sweet & Maxwell, 1977)

Dictionnaire des Termes Juridiques (Editions de Vecchi, 1986)

WT/DS34/AB/R

The New Shorter Oxford English Dictionary (Clarendon Press, 1993)

WT/DS46/AB/R

Black's Law Dictionary (West Publishing Co., 1990)

The New Shorter Oxford English Dictionary (Clarendon Press, 1993)

WT/DS50/AB/R

The Concise Oxford English Dictionary (1990)

WT/DS60/AB/R

The Shorter Oxford English Dictionary (Guild Publishing, 1983)

WT/DS69/AB/R

The Dictionary of Trade Policy Terms (Centre for International Economic Studies, 1998)

Dictionary of International Trade (World Trade Press, 1998)

WT/DS70/AB/R

Black's Law Dictionary (West Publishing Co. 1990)

The New Shorter Oxford English Dictionary (Clarendon Press, 1993)

The Concise Oxford Dictionary (Clarendon Press, 1995)

Webster's Third New International Dictionary (William Benton, 1966)

WT/DS75/AB/R, WT/DS84/AB/R

The New Shorter Oxford English Dictionary (Clarendon Press, 1993)

Webster's Dictionary

The Concise Oxford Dictionary

WT/DS76/AB/R

The Shorter Oxford English Dictionary, Third Edition (1983)

WT/DS90/AB/R

The New Shorter Oxford English Dictionary (Clarendon Press, 1993)

The Concise Oxford English Dictionary (Clarendon Press, 1995)

WT/DS98/AB/R

Webster's Third New International Dictionary (Encyclopedia Britannica Inc., 1966)

Black's Law Dictionary, 6th ed. (West Publishing Company, 1990)

WT/DS103/AB/R, WT/DS113/AB/R

Black's Law Dictionary (West Publishing Co., 1990)

The New Shorter Oxford English Dictionary, Lesley Brown (ed.) (Clarendon Press, 1993) Merriam Webster's Collegiate Dictionary (Merriam Webster Inc., 1993)

The Shorter Oxford English Dictionary, C.T. Onions (ed.) (Guild Publishing, 1983)

WT/DS108/AB/R

Webster's Third International Dictionary

The New Shorter Oxford English Dictionary, Lesley Brown (ed.) (Clarendon Press, 1993)

WT/DS121/AB/R

Black's Law Dictionary (West Publishing Co., 5th ed., 1979)

Webster's Third New International Dictionary (Encyclopedia Britannica Inc., 1966)

Black's Law Dictionary, 6th ed. (West Publishing Company, 1990)

WT/DS122/AB/R

Concise Oxford Dictionary

Black's Law Dictionary

The New Shorter Oxford English Dictionary (Clarendon Press, 1993)

WT/DS135/AB/R

The New Shorter Oxford English Dictionary, Lesley Brown (ed.) (Clarendon Press, 1993)

WT/DS141/AB/R

The Concise Oxford Dictionary of Current English (Clarendon Press, 1995)

The New Shorter Oxford English Dictionary (Clarendon Press, 1993)

Black's Law Dictionary (West Group, 1999)

WT/DS161/AB/R, WT/DS169/AB/R

The New Shorter Oxford English Dictionary (Clarendon Press, 1993)

The Concise Oxford English Dictionary (Clarendon Press, 1995)

Black's Law Dictionary, (West Publishing, 1995)

WT/DS166/AB/R

The New Shorter Oxford English Dictionary (Brown, ed.) (Clarendon Press, 1993)

WT/DS170/AB/R

Black's Law Dictionary

The New Shorter Oxford English Dictionary, Lesley Brown (ed.) (Clarendon Press, 1993)

WT/DS176/AB/R

The New Shorter Oxford English Dictionary, L. Brown (ed.) (Clarendon Press, 1993)

Le Petit Robert Dictionnaire de la Langue Française (1995)

Black's Law Dictionary, 7th ed., B.A. Garner (ed.), (West Group, 1999)

WT/DS184/AB/R

The New Shorter Oxford English Dictionary, Lesley Brown (ed.) (Clarendon Press, 1993)

Black's Law Dictionary, 6th ed. (1990)

WT/DS192/AB/R

The New Shorter Oxford English Dictionary, L. Brown (ed.) (Clarendon Press, 1993)

WT/DS202/AB/R

The New Shorter Oxford English Dictionary, L. Brown (ed.) (Clarendon Press, 1993)

WT/DS207/AB/R

The New Shorter Oxford Dictionary, L. Brown (ed.) (Clarendon Press), 1993

WT/DS217/AB/R ,WT/DS234/AB/R

New Shorter Oxford English Dictionary

WT/DS231/AB/R

The New Shorter Oxford English Dictionary on Historical Principles (Clarendon Press)

Webster's New World Dictionary (William Collins & World Publishing Co., Inc., 1976)

The New Shorter Oxford English Dictionary (Clarendon Press, 1993)

The Multilingual Illustrated Dictionary of Aquatic Animals and Plants

Grand Dictionnaire Encyclopédique Larousse

Diccionario de la lengua española

WT/DS244/AB/R

Shorter Oxford English Dictionary, 5th ed., W.R. Trumble, A. Stevenson (eds.) (Oxford University Press, 2002)

WT/DS245/AB/R

Shorter Oxford English Dictionary, 5th ed., W.R. Trumble, A. Stevenson (eds.) (Oxford University Press, 2002)

WT/DS246/AB/R

Shorter Oxford English Dictionary, 5th ed., W.R. Trumble, A. Stevenson (eds.) (Oxford University Press, 2002)

The New Shorter Oxford English Dictionary, L. Brown (ed.) (Clarendon Press, 1993)

WT/DS248/AB/R , WT/DS249/AB/R , WT/DS251/AB/R , WT/DS252/AB/R , WT/DS253/AB/R ,WT/DS254/AB/R, WT/DS258/AB/R, WT/DS259/AB/R

New Shorter Oxford English Dictionary, L. Brown (ed.) (Clarendon Press, 1993)

Shorter Oxford English Dictionary, 5th ed. W.R. Trumble, A. Stevenson (eds.) (Oxford University Press, 2002)

WT/DS257/AB/R

Black's Law Dictionary, 7th ed., B.A. Garner (ed.) (West Group, 1999)

The New Shorter Oxford Dictionary, L. Brown (ed.) (Clarendon Press, 1993), Vol. I,

Shorter Oxford English Dictionary, 5th ed., W.R. Trumble, A. Stevenson (eds.) (Oxford University Press, 2002)

Collins Dictionary of the English Language, G.A. Wilkes (ed.) (Wm. Collins Publishing, 1979)

WT/DS264/AB/R

Shorter Oxford English Dictionary, 5th ed., W.R. Trumble, A. Stevenson (eds.) (Oxford University Press, 2002)

WT/DS267/AB/R

The New Shorter Oxford English Dictionary (1993)

Merriam-Webster Dictionary online

Shorter Oxford English Dictionary, 5th ed., W.R. Trumble, A. Stevenson (eds.) (Oxford University Press, 2002)

WT/DS268/AB/R

Collins Dictionary of the English Language, G.A. Wilkes (ed.) (Wm. Collins Publishing, 1979)

WT/DS276/AB/R

The New Shorter Oxford English Dictionary, L. Brown (ed.) (Clarendon Press 1993)

Shorter Oxford English Dictionary, 5th ed., W.R. Trumble, A. Stevenson (eds.) (Oxford University Press, 2002)

WT/DS282/AB/R

The New Shorter Oxford English Dictionary, L. Brown (ed.) (Clarendon Press, 1993)

WT/DS285/AB/R

The Shorter Oxford English Dictionary

The New Shorter Oxford English Dictionary

WT/DS286/AB/R

Shorter Oxford English Dictionary, 5th edn, W.R. Trumble, A. Stevenson (eds) (Oxford University Press, 2002)

WT/DS294/AB/R

The New Shorter Oxford English Dictionary, L. Brown (ed.) (Clarendon Press, 1993)

WT/DS296/AB/R

The New Shorter Oxford English Dictionary, L. Brown (ed.) (Clarendon Press, 1993)

Black's Law Dictionary, 7th edn, B.A. Garner (ed.) (West Group, 1999)

Oxford Dictionary of English, C. Soanes and A. Stevenson (eds) (Oxford University Press, 2004)

Shorter Oxford English Dictionary, 5th edn, W.R. Trumble, A. Stevenson (eds) (Oxford University Press, 2002)

WT/DS308/AB/R

The Concise Oxford English Dictionary (Clarendon Press, 1995)

Black's Law Dictionary (1990)

WT/DS320/AB/R

Shorter Oxford English Dictionary, 5th edition (1993)

The New Shorter Oxford English Dictionary, 4th edn, L. Brown (ed.) (Clarendon Press, 1993)

The New Shorter Oxford English Dictionary, 1990

Merriam-Webster Medical Dictionary available at: www.merriam-webster.com

WT/DS321/AB/R

Shorter Oxford English Dictionary, 5th edition (1993)

The New Shorter Oxford English Dictionary, 4th edn, L. Brown (ed.) (Clarendon Press, 1993)

The New Shorter Oxford English Dictionary, 1990

Merriam-Webster Medical Dictionary available at: <www.merriam-webster.com>)

WT/DS336/AB/R

The New Shorter Oxford English Dictionary, L. Brown (ed.) (Clarendon Press, 1993)

Concise Oxford English Dictionary, 10th ed., (Oxford, 2002)

WT/DS339/AB/R, WT/DS340/AB/R, WT/DS342/AB/R

The New Shorter Oxford English Dictionary, 4th edn, L. Brown (ed.) (Clarendon Press, 1993)

WT/DS345/AB/R

The New Shorter Oxford English Dictionary, 4th edn, L. Brown (ed.) (Clarendon Press, 1993)

WT/DS360/AB/R

Shorter Oxford English Dictionary, 5th edn, W.R. Trumble, A. Stevenson (eds) (Oxford University Press, 2002)

Black's Law Dictionary, 7th edn, B.A. Garner (ed.) (West Group, 1999)

WT/DS363/AB/R

The American Heritage Dictionary of the English Language

WT/DS367/AB/R

Shorter Oxford English Dictionary, 6th edn, A. Stevenson (ed.) (Oxford University Press, 2007)

WT/DS379/AB/R

Shorter Oxford English Dictionary, 6th edn, A. Stevenson (ed.) (Oxford University Press, 2007)

資料3　WTOパネル報告書において辞書を利用して意味を確定した用語一覧

WT/DS8/R, WT/DS10/R, WT/DS11/R

so as, so as to

WT/DS18/R

potential, probability, likelihood

WT/DS27/R

manner

WT/DS33/R

good faith

WT/DS34/R

substantially, trade

WT/DS44/R

measure

WT/DS46/R

benefit, obtain, material, advantage, field, phase out, gradually, advantage, grant, potential, proceeding, proceedings

WT/DS48/R

base, consistency

WT/DS50/R

exclusive

WT/DS54/R, WT/DS55/R, WT/DS59/R, WT/DS64/R

displace, effect, serious

WT/DS56/R

presumption

WT/DS69/R

base

WT/DS70/R

finance, confer, benefit, advantage

WT/DS75/R, WT/DS84/R

distillation, potential, expectation

WT/DS76/R

variety, nectarine

WT/DS79/R

directory provision

WT/DS90/R

application, thereupon, restriction

WT/DS98/R

immediately

WT/DS99/R

warranted, burden of proof, case

WT/DS103/R, WT/DS113/R

payment, remunerate, benefit, mandate, mandated, consumer, consume, provide, represents, payments-in-kind, circumvent, entrust

WT/DS108/R

sanctity, processes, activity, refer, instrument, provide, economic, evidence, available, statement, due, decision, marketing, grant

WT/DS114/R

limited, enjoyment, normal, legitimate, unreasonable, exploit

WT/DS121/R

application, clarity

WT/DS122/R

notify, positive, consider, significant, such as, include, including, evaluate, fact, objective, unbiased, may

WT/DS126/R

grant, benefit, evidence, provision, conditioned, anticipate, available, statement, contingent

WT/DS132/R

demonstrate

WT/DS135/R

characteristic, asbestos, document, process, method, standard

WT/DS136/R

discrimination, legislative history, interlocutory, may

WT/DS138/R

enterprise, arm's length transaction, fair market value, offset, benefit, to deter

WT/DS139/R, WT/DS142/R

condition, unconditional, benefit, undertake, advantage, all, contingent, requirements, revenue, due, law, delay

WT/DS141/R

such as, remedy, explore, average, weighted, basis, actual, evaluation, impact, examination, constructive

WT/DS146/R, WT/DS175/R

importation, requirement, inherent, res judicata, on

WT/DS152/R

rule, ensure, shall, determine, discretion, mandatory, directory provision, determination

WT/DS155/R

uniform, necessary, discrimination, charge

WT/DS156/R

commence, independence, investigation, increase, immediately, should

WT/DS160/R

certain, special, case, exploit, normal, interests, prejudice, reasonable

WT/DS161/R, WT/DS169/R

procedure, eligible, charge, restriction, remain, result

WT/DS162/R

discrimination, legislative history, interlocutory, may

WT/DS163/R

entity, agent, prescribe, prescription, subordinate, a separate legal entity, of a corporation, essential, define, include, branch

WT/DS165/R

seeking, to seek, redress, determination, retaliation, sanction

WT/DS166/R

representative, immediately, necessary, emergency measures

WT/DS170/R

available, subject matter, acts, unwarranted

WT/DS174/R

concern, interest, prejudice, separate

WT/DS176/R

in respect of, subject matter, other, ground, derogate, as is, telle quelle, available, substantiate, owner, le titulaire, el titular

WT/DS177/R, WT/DS178/R

unforeseen, producer, produce, product, output, cause, allegation, conjecture, possibility, imminent, necessary, unexpected, to demonstrate, to discern, least, link, endeavor, production

WT/DS179/R

between, term, condition, comparable, terms of sale

WT/DS184/R

cooperate, reasonable, sufficient, evidence, believe, suspect, to focus, primary, circumspection, withhold, ordinary course of business, whole, impartial, uniform, adverse, favourable, adverse inference rule, special, would, determine

WT/DS189/R

inform, essential, consideration, whether

WT/DS192/R

produce, competitive, serious damage, yam count, justifiable

WT/DS194/R

entrust, directs, to carry out, direct, body, type

WT/DS202/R

tariff quota, fix, specify, is being imported

WT/DS204/R

telecommunications facilities, transmission facility, link, interconnect, interconnection, practices, competitive, appropriate, reasonable, necessary, to orient

WT/DS206/R

remedy, information, necessary, all, take into account, verifiable, verify, appropriately, undue, explore, proper, should, withhold, operationalize, fair, explored, category, affidavit, verification

WT/DS207/R

ordinary, similar, to publish, variable levies, clear, variable import levy

WT/DS211/R

evaluation, having a bearing on , to the best of one's ability, best, reasonable, known

WT/DS213/R

determine

WT/DS217/R, WT/DS234/R

against, response, in particular, economic, offset, counteract

WT/DS219/R

warrant, remedy, determine, appropriate, suitable, fitting, evaluate, having a bearing on , material, regard, explore, proper, objective, investigate, whether, that, competition, condition

資料3　WTOパネル報告書において辞書を利用して意味を確定した用語一覧

WT/DS221/R

bring

WT/DS222/R

benefit, anticipated, letter of comfort, letter of awareness

WT/DS231/R

sardines, name, label, relevant, imminent, as a basis, performance, use, ineffective, inappropriate, to pursue

WT/DS236/R

provides, goods, in relation to, provide, good, prevailing, timber

WT/DS238/R

context

WT/DS241/R

major, estoppels, when, participate, provide, reason, actual, facilitar, evidence, comparable, compare, simultaneous, satisfied, promptly, objective, subjective, proportion, major part, majority, res judicata, estoppel, simultaneously, essential, fact, majeur, statement

WT/DS243/R

instrument, create, have, restrictive, distorting, disruptive, used, as instrument, to pursue, strict, unduly, circumvention, drill, circumventing, transship, objective, disrupt, distortion, disrupts

WT/DS244/R

determine, unless, mutatis mutandis, likely, de facto, to initiate, procedural, continuation, recurrence, own, initiative, procedure

WT/DS245/R

evidence

WT/DS246/R

non-discriminatory, positive right, the, notwithstanding, discriminate, exception, statutory exception, unconditional, advantage, generalize, unconditionally, affirmative defence, special exception, conditional right, discriminatory tariff, non-discriminatory tariff, generaliser, general

WT/DS248/R, WT/DS249/R, WT/DS251/R, WT/DS252/R, WT/DS253/R, WT/DS254/R, WT/DS258/R, WT/DS259/R

result, development, product, like, rate, emergency, coincide, nature, extent, negligible, important, facilitate, increased, increase, prevent, remedy, adjustment, source, impartial, reasonable, uniform causal, cause

WT/DS257/R

goods, provides, good, adequate, prevailing, timely, to inform, in relation to, limited, property, licence, industry, offset, guideline

WT/DS264/R

basis, general, administrative, pertain, characteristic, close, resemble, fair, general costs, G & A

WT/DS265/R, WT/DS266/R, WT/DS283/R

silence, estoppels by, commitments, on

WT/DS267/R

commodity, notwithstanding, exempt, action, proceeding, related, base, decide, grant, specific, premiums, inadequate, cover, long-term, operating, operate, cost, losses, circumvent, industry, price, suppress, depression, significant, may, serious, market, share, include

WT/DS268/R

determination, likely, probable, whole, also, mutatis mutandis, imminent, major proportion, review, determine, expeditions, irrefutable, uniform, impartial, reasonable, continuation, likely, procedure, ensure, continuation, recurrence, any

WT/DS269/R

salted, to salt, in brine, dried, smoked, non liquet situation, preserve, to prepare, process, fresh, chilled, frozen, freeze, cure

WT/DS273/R

public body, entrust, direct, depression, suppress, public, substantial, practice, programme, may, illustrative

WT/DS276/R

identify, undertake, commercial, distribution, rational, shall, will, use

WT/DS277/R

special, care, vulnerable, consider, circumstance

WT/DS282/R

determine, any, likely, consider, rely

WT/DS285/R

sporting, gamble, to bet, gambling, enterainment, recreational, none, limitations, market access, public, order, recreation, form, express, designate, moral, necessary ,numerical, quota

WT/DS291/R, WT/DS292/R, WT/DS293/R

suspension, de facto, summary, brief, weeds, procedure, moratorium, failure, to arise from, additives, damage, trophic, fauna, organism, pest, disease, food, substance, contaminant, toxin, mycotoxin, microbial toxin, mycotoxins, allergen, biodiversity, undue, delay, take account of, undertake, complete, standard, potential, review, ordinance, exempt, evaluate

WT/DS294/R

investigation, existence, phase, the, procedure, fair

WT/DS295/R

best, known, to investigate, investigator, offset, prevent

WT/DS296/R

entrust, direct, body, use, investigate, link, relationship

WT/DS299/R

entrust, direct, significant, output

WT/DS301/R

redress, determination, matters, against, seeking, to seek

WT/DS302/R

arbitrary, unjustifiable, detriment, restriction, original, on, reasonable

WT/DS308/R

laws, regulations, apply, compliance, comply, secure, international agreement

WT/DS312/R

product, consider

WT/DS315/R

administer, execute, uniform, uniformity, fair, transparency, transparent, at issue, manner, administration, process, aplicar, appliquer, apply, general, application, shall, acrylate, classification, valuation, entry, audit, penalties, record-keeping, release, govern, independent, pertaining to, discretion

WT/DS320/R

measure, scientific, science, critical, critical size, critical mass, potential, possibility, arise, deliberation, endocrine system, endocrinology, endogenous, epidemiology, good faith, adequate, insufficient

WT/DS321/R

complaint, measure, scienfitic, science, critical, critical size, critical mass, potential, possibility, arise, deliberation, endocrine system, endocrinology, endogenous, epidemiology, good faith, adequate, insufficient

WT/DS322/R

comparison, fair, investigation, administrative, procedure, phase

資料３　WTOパネル報告書において辞書を利用して意味を確定した用語一覧

WT/DS332/R

arbitrary, unjustifiable, justifiable, accumulate, accumulation, to exempt

WT/DS334/R

requirement, rice, licence, discretionary, invest

WT/DS335/R

rational, examine

WT/DS336/R

method, transfer, funds, interested parties, interested

WT/DS337/R

produce, determine, cost, appropriate, actual, or, verifiable, production, fact

WT/DS341/R

formally, commence, invite, due, restraint, producer, establish, produce, producers, crear, création, establishment

WT/DS339/R, WT/DS340/R, WT/DS342/R

internal taxes, importation, on, circumvention, anti-circumvention, tax avoidance, tax evasion, kit, whole, part, customs duties, ordinary, circumvent, screwdrive operations, as presented, consignment, split, SKD, motor, vehicle, car

WT/DS343/R

typically, suspected, duty, reasonableness, to, necessary

WT/DS345/R

obiter dictum, suspected, reasonableness, duty, reasonable, necessary

WT/DS350/R

investigation, fair, price, during, existence, the

WT/DS360/R

equivalent, ordinary, charge, equality, equal in force

WT/DS362/R

shall, scale, authority, disposal, dispose, principles, avoid, simple, exceptional, commercial

WT/DS363/R

distribution, unify, subscription, digital, recording, material, recorded material, commodity, product, record, video, entertainment, software, distributor, without prejudice, regulate, import, related to, including, include, discretionary, audiovisual, 电影, audio, visual, distribution channel, consumer, importation

WT/DS366/R

value, levy, guarantee, payment, restriction, freedom, transit, valuation

WT/DS367/R

requirement, procedure, negligible, undertake, complete

WT/DS375/R, WT/DS376/R, WT/DS377/R

mutatis mutandis, classify, involved, for, flat panel display devices, an electronic display, LCD display, panel, devices, set top box, modem, publish, bring about, uniform, printer, intermediate, photocopying, xerography, display, output units

WT/DS379/R

commercial, public, government, body, private enterprise, public sector,appropriate, questionnaire, controlling interest, commercial

WT/DS383/R

equitativo

WT/DS392/R

arbitrary, approval, indication, ban, unjustifiable, justifiable, approving, authorization, elaborate

資料3　WTOパネル報告書において辞書を利用して意味を確定した用語一覧

WT/DS397/R

potential, questionnaire, several, impracticable

WT/DS399/R

contribute, cause, rapidly, significant, rapid, recent, contribuer, disruption, causer, causar, causa, remedy, increase, may

資料4　WTO上級委員会報告書において辞書を利用して意味を確定した用語一覧

WT/DS2/AB/R

made effective, in conjunction with

WT/DS18/AB/R

likelihood

WT/DS26/AB/R

based on, conform to, potential, probability, scientific, science

WT/DS27/AB/R

standing, locus standi

WT/DS33/AB/R

burden of proof

WT/DS34/AB/R

shall not prevent

WT/DS46/AB/R

to grant, proceeding, proceedings

WT/DS50/AB/R

conceder

WT/DS60/AB/R

matter

WT/DS69/AB/R

global annual tariff quota

WT/DS70/AB/R

benefit, anticipated, proceeding, confer, contingent, tie, should

WT/DS75/AB/R, WT/DS84/AB/R

basic rationale, compatitive, substitutable

WT/DS76/AB/R

sufficient

WT/DS90/AB/R

arise, application, thereupon

WT/DS98/AB/R

unforeseen, unforeseeable

WT/DS103/AB/R, WT/DS113/AB/R

government, payment, consumer

WT/DS108/AB/R

provide, marketing, commitments, circumvent

WT/DS121/AB/R

unforeseen, de novo review

WT/DS122/AB/R

positive evidence, objective, establishment, proper

WT/DS135/AB/R

like

WT/DS141/AB/R

comparable, average, to weight, weighted average, realized

WT/DS161/AB/R, WT/DS169/AB/R

necessary

WT/DS166/AB/R

all, investigation, cause, attribute, bearing

WT/DS170/AB/R

available, subject matter

WT/DS176/AB/R

as is, telle quelle, derogate, owner, available, substantiate

WT/DS184/AB/R

cooperate, focus, primarily

WT/DS192/AB/R

competitive, by

WT/DS202/AB/R

or, discrete

WT/DS207/AB/R

similar, ordinary, convert, levy, propiamente dicho, proprement dit

WT/DS217/AB/R ,WT/DS234/AB/R

against

WT/DS231/AB/R

based on, basis, ineffective, inappropriate, sardines

WT/DS244/AB/R

determine

WT/DS245/AB/R

might

WT/DS246/AB/R

non-discriminatory preference, accordance, notwithstanding, discriminate, generalized, positive

WT/DS248/AB/R, WT/DS249/AB/R, WT/DS251/AB/R, WT/DS252/AB/R, WT/DS253/AB/R, WT/DS254/AB/R, WT/DS258/AB/R, WT/DS259/AB/R

result, reason, conclusion

WT/DS257/AB/R

goods, provides, adequate, remuneration, in relation to, prevailing, as regards, rapport, respect

WT/DS264/AB/R

consider

WT/DS267/AB/R

market, support to a , specific commodity, grant, decide, defined and fixed base period, related to, base, specific, effect

WT/DS268/AB/R

ample

WT/DS276/AB/R

enterprise, participation

WT/DS282/AB/R

any

WT/DS285/AB/R

sporting, recreational, entertainment, form, numerical, quota

WT/DS286/AB/R

salted, dried, smoked, in brine, brine, to dry, to smoke

WT/DS294/AB/R

investigation

WT/DS296/AB/R

entrust, direct, probative, compelling, determine

WT/DS308/AB/R

should, laws, regulations

WT/DS315/AB/R

administer

WT/DS320/AB/R

critical mass, removed, authorized, proceedings, deliberations, latency period

WT/DS321/AB/R

critical mass, removed, authorized, proceedings, deliberations, latency period

WT/DS336/AB/R

provided for, method

WT/DS339/AB/R, WT/DS340/AB/R, WT/DS342/AB/R

as, presented

WT/DS345/AB/R

reasonable, certain, suspected, likely

WT/DS360/AB/R

equivalent, ejusdem generis, qua

WT/DS363/AB/R

distribution, recording, commodity, distribution channel, videos, without prejudice to, right, regulate, trade

WT/DS367/AB/R

to, delay, undue

WT/DS379/AB/R

public body, private enterprise, public sector, organism, público, organisme, public, appropriate, government, direct, entrust, direction, entrustment, explicitly, express, certain, group, enterprise, industry, comparable, commercial, amount

参考文献

◆外国語参考文献

Bradly J. Condon, Lost in Translation: A comparative Analysis of Plurilingual Interpretation in WTO Panel and Appellate Body Reports

Chang-Fa Lo, Good Faith Use of Dictionary in the Search of Ordinary Meaning under the WTO Dispute Settlement Understanding, Journal of International Dispute Settlement, Vol. 1, No.2 (2010)

Changfa Lo,J. Int. Disp. Settlement (2011), first published online July 23, 2011 doi:10.1093/jnlids/idr013

David Palmeter and Petros C.Mavroidis, Dispute Settlement in the World Trade Organization 2nd.ed.Cambridge University Press (2004)

Ernst-Ulrich Petersmann, Tribute: On the Constitution of John Jackson, 20 Mich. J. Int'l L. 149 (1999)

Howard Jackson, Lexicography: An Introduction, Taylor & Francis Routledge, (2002)（南出康世＝石川慎一郎『英語辞書学への招待』大修館書店（2004年））

Isabelle Van Damme, Journal of International Dispute Settlement, Vol. 2, No. 1 (2011)

Isabelle Van Damme, Treaty Interpretation by the WTO Appellate Body, Eur. J. Int. Law 21 (3) (2010)

Jeffrey L. Kirchmeier Samuel Thumma, Scaling the Lexicon Fortress: The United States Supreme Court's Use of Dictionaries in the Twenty-First Century, Marquette Law Review, Vol. 94 (2010)

John H. Jackson, Sovereignty, the WTO, and Changing Fundamentals of International Law, Cambridge University Press (2006)

John H. Jackson, The Jurisprudence of GATT & the WTO, Cam-

bridge University Press (2007)
Merriam-Webster's Collegiate Dictionary 10th ed. (2001)
Phillip A. Rubin, War of the Words: How Courts Can Use Dictionaries in accordance with Textualist Principles, Duke Law Journal, Vol. 60 (2010)
Roderick Munday, The Bridge That Choked a Watercourse or Repetitive Dictionary Disorder, 29 STATUTE L.REV.26,32 (2008)
The Shorter Oxford English Dictionary (2002)
The Webster's New Encyclopedic Dictionary (2003)
Webster's New World Dictionary of American English (1993)
Yearbook of the International Law Commission Vol. I (1966)
Yearbook of the International Law Commission Vol. II (1966)

◆日本語参考文献

「日本貿易振興機構（JETRO）中国の完成車特徴認定制度」及び「完成車の特徴を構成する自動車部品輸入管理弁法」日本貿易振興機構（JETRO）
『2011年版不公正貿易報告』経済産業省通商政策局
奥脇直也『国際条約集』(有斐閣，2009年)
坂元茂樹『条約法の理論と実際』(東信堂，2004年)
菊地正「国際条約の解釈──原文に基づく方法──」名城法学（1972年12月）2巻1・2号
清水章雄「ガットの紛争処理手続き」商学討究34巻2号（小樽商科大学，1983年)
清水章雄「WTO紛争解決における解釈手法の展開と問題点」日本国際経済法学会年報第19号（法律文化社，2010年)
山手治之「条約の解釈」立命館法学48巻（1962年)
山形英郎「国際司法裁判所における条約解釈手段の展開──ヴァッテル規則からの脱却」日本国際経済法学会年報第19号（法律文化社，2010年)

山形英郎「条約の解釈とは何か」法学セミナー（2010年1月）
山形英郎「条約解釈目的と条約解釈手段――条約解釈規則の誕生――」法学雑誌（2010年3月）56巻3・4号
松下満雄「米国の国境を越えた賭博サービスの及ぼす影響に係る措置」上級委員会報告」ガット・WTOの紛争処理に関する調査調査報告書XVI（2005年）
松下満雄＝清水章雄＝中川淳司『ガット・WTO法』（有斐閣，2000年）
松下満雄＝清水章雄＝中川淳司『ケースブック：WTO法』（有斐閣，2009年）
土屋裕明「多数国間条約に対する解釈宣言と条約の解釈」国際関係論研究（1996年10月）
小寺彰＝中川淳司『基本経済条約集』（有斐閣，2009年）
佐分晴夫「WTOレジームの現段階――ケースを中心として――」日本国際経済法学会年報第8号（法律文化社，1999年）
佐藤弘『英語辞書の実際』（八潮出版社，1982年）

◆ GATTパネル報告書

GATT Panel Report, Anti-Dumping Duties on Imports of Polyacetal Resins from the United States, ADP/92, 2 April 1993
GATT Panel Report, EEC Restrictions on Imports of Apples from Chile, L/5047, BISD 27S/98, 10 November 1980
GATT Panel Report, United States - Imposition of Anti-dumping Duties on Imports of Fresh and Chilled Atlantic Salmon From Norway, ADP/87, 27 April 1994
GATT Panel Report, United States - Imposition of Countervailing Duties on Imports of Fresh and Chilled Atlantic Salmon From Norway, SCM/153, 28 April 1994
GATT Panel Report, United States - Measures Affecting Imports of Softwood Lumber from Canada, SCM/162, 27 October 1993
GATT Panel Report, United States - Imposition of Countervailing

Duties on Certain Hot-Rolled Lead and Bismuth Carbon Steel Products Originating in France, Germany and the United Kingdom, SCM/185, 15 November 1994

◆ WTO パネル報告書

Report of the panel, United States - Standards for Reformulated and Conventional Gasoline, WT/DS2/R, 29 January 1996

Report of the Panel, Japan - Taxes on Alcoholic Beverages, WT/DS8/R; WT/DS10/R; WT/DS11/R, 11 July 1996

Report of the Panel, India - Measures Affecting the Automotive Sector, WT/DS146/R; WT/DS175/R, 21 December 2001

Report of the Panel, United States - Safeguard Measures on Imports of Fresh, Chilled of Frozen Lamb Meat from New Zealand and Australia, WT/DS177/R; WT/DS178/R,21 December 2000

Report of the Panel, United States - Continued Dumping and Subsidy Offset Act of 2000, WT/DS217/R; WT/DS234/R, 16 September 2002

Report of the Panel, European Communities - Export Subsidies on Sugar Complaint by Australia, WT/DS265/R, 15 October 2004

Report of the Panel, United States - Final Countervailing Duty Determination with Respect to Certain Softwood Lumber from Canada, WT/DS257/R, 29 August 2003

Report of the Panel, United States - Measures Affecting the Cross-Border Supply of Gambling and Betting Service, WT/DS285/R, 10 November 2004

Report of the Panel, United States - Laws, Regulations and Methodology for Calculating Dumping Margins ("Zeroing"), WT/DS294/R, 31 October 2005

Report of the Panel, Dominican Republic – Measures Affecting the Importation and Internal Sale of Cigarettes, WT/DS302/R, 26 November 2004

Reports of the Panel, China - Measures Affecting Imports of Automobile Parts WT/DS339/R; WT/DS340R; WT/DS342/R, 18 July 2008

Report of the Panel, China - Measures Affecting Trading Rights and Distribution Services for Certain Publications and Audiovisual Entertainment Products, WT/DS363/R, 12 August 2009

Report of the Panel, European Communities and its Member States Tariff Treatment of Certain Information Technology Products, WT/DS375/R; WT/DS376/R; WT/DS377/R, 16 August 2010

Report of the Panel, United States - Definitive Anti-Dumping and Countervailing Duties on Certain Products from China, WT/DS379/R, 22 October 2010

◆ WTO 上級委員会報告書

Report of the Appellate Body, United States - Standards for Reformulated and Conventional Gasoline, WT/DS2/AB/R, 29 April 1996

Report of the Appellate Body Japan - Taxes on Alcoholic Beverages, WT/DS8/AB/R; WT/DS10/AB/R; WT/DS11/AB/R, 4 October 1996

Report of the Appellate Body, India - Patent Protection For Pharmaceutical And Agricultural Chemical Products, WT/DS50/AB/R, 19 December 1997

Report of the Appellate Body, Canada – Measures Affecting the Export of Civilian Aircraft, WT/DS70/AB/R, 2 August 1999

Report of the Appellate Body, United States - Tax Treatment for "Foreign Sales Corporations", WT/DS108/AB/R, 24 February 2000

Report of the Appellate Body, Thailand - Anti-Dumping Duties on Angles, Shapes and Sections of Iron Or Non-alloy Steel and H-

Beams from Poland, WT/DS122/AB/R, 12 March 2001

Report of the Appellate Body, European Communities - Measures Affecting Asbestos And Asbestos-Containing Products, WT/DS135/AB/R, 12 March 2001

Report of the Appellate Body, Chile – Price Band System and Safeguard Measures Relating to Certain Agricultural Products Recourse to Article 21.5 of the DSU by Argentina, WT/DS207/AB/RW, 7 May 2007

Report of the Appellate Body, United States - Continued Dumping and Subsidy Offset Act of 2000, WT/DS217/AB/R; WT/DS234/AB/R, 16 January 2003

Report of the Appellate Body, United States - Final Countervailing Duty Determination with Respect to Certain Softwood Lumber from Canada, WT/DS257/AB/R, 19 January 2004

Report of the Appellate Body, European Communities - Customs Classification of Frozen Boneless Chicken Cuts, WT/DS269/AB/R; WT/DS286/AB/R, 12 September 2005

Report of the Appellate Body, United States - Measures Affecting the Cross-Border Supply of Gambling and Betting Service, WT/DS285/AB/R, 7 April 2005

Report of the Appellate Body, United States - Countervailing Duty Investigation on Dynamic Random Access Memory Semiconductors (Drams) From Korea, WT/DS296/AB/R, 27 June 2005

Report Of The Appellate Body, China - Measures Affecting Trading Rights and Distribution Services for Certain Publications and Audiovisual Entertainment Products, WT/DS363/AB/R, 21 December 2009

事件索引

事 項 索 引

〈著者紹介〉

袁　　田（エン　デン）

1978年生まれ．

2000年　中国北京第二外国語大学スペイン語学部卒業．

2000年　中国上海招商局国際旅行会社，台湾年興集団(ニカラグア)，
　　　　中国華立集団等を経て，退職．

2007年　中国司法試験合格

2010年　東京大学総合法政専攻入学

2012年　同卒業

現　在　中国上海市光明法律事務所

信山社双書
実際編

WTO紛争処理の一断面
──協定解釈と「辞書」の利用──

2012(平成24)年8月3日　第1版第1刷発行

著　者　袁　　　田
発行者　今井　貴・稲葉文子
発行所　㈱　信　山　社
〒113-0033 東京都文京区本郷6-2-9-102
TEL 03-3818-1019　FAX 03-3818-0344
Printed in Japan　info@shinzansha.co.jp

印刷・製本／東洋印刷・渋谷文泉閣

出版契約No.2012-1123-8-01011
ISBN 978-4-7972-1123-8 C3332
1123-012-0120-030
NDC 分類 329.601-d006